MW01100723

REMARQUE

ALL QUIET ON THE WESTERN FRONT

NOTES

COLES EDITORIAL BOARD

Bound to stay open

Publisher's Note

Otabind (Ota-bind). This book has been bound using the patented Otabind process. You can open this book at any page, gently run your finger down the spine, and the pages will lie flat.

ABOUT COLES NOTES

COLES NOTES have been an indispensible aid to students on five continents since 1948.

COLES NOTES are available for a wide range of individual literary works. Clear, concise explanations and insights are provided along with interesting interpretations and evaluations.

Proper use of COLES NOTES will allow the student to pay greater attention to lectures and spend less time taking notes. This will result in a broader understanding of the work being studied and will free the student for increased participation in discussions.

COLES NOTES are an invaluable aid for review and exam preparation as well as an invitation to explore different interpretive paths.

COLES NOTES are written by experts in their fields. It should be noted that any literary judgement expressed herein is just that — the judgement of one school of thought. Interpretations that diverge from, or totally disagree with any criticism may be equally valid.

COLES NOTES are designed to supplement the text and are not intended as a substitute for reading the text itself. Use of the NOTES will serve not only to clarify the work being studied, but should enhance the reader's enjoyment of the topic.

ISBN 0-7740-3491-2

© COPYRIGHT 1992 AND PUBLISHED BY
COLES PUBLISHING COMPANY
TORONTO—CANADA
PRINTED IN CANADA

Manufactured by Webcom Limited
Cover finish: Webcom's Exclusive **Duracoat**

CONTENTS

Erich Maria Remarque: Life and Works

Erich Maria Remarque was born on June 22, 1898 in Osnabrück, Germany. His father, a bookbinder, was German, but his mother was of French ancestry. As a child, Remarque went through the ordinary school system of his time, including the gymnasium (elementary school), then the stadium (high school) and, finally, the University of Münster.

At the age of 18, while still a student at university, Remarque was drafted into the German army. He fought in World War I at the Western Front (see summary of WWI) and was injured five times. His last wound was quite serious.

During the war, Remarque developed a hostility for warlike activities and a resentment toward the older generation that had catapulted his country into the war. His anger and frustration built up during the post-war years and culminated in his first novel, *All Quiet on the Western Front* (1929).

In the years before publishing this novel, he found that life was difficult. The war had made a permanent impact on the lives of people and had caused a reorganization of traditional life-styles. For a while, he worked as a teacher. But his restlessness prompted him to seek work as a stonecutter in a local cemetery. All of his experiences eventually found their way into his novels, and this work as a stonecutter paved the way for his 1957 novel, *The Black Obelisk*.

His cemetery work led to a period of travel with a gypsy caravan. They wandered throughout Germany for a time, then he became a test driver for a Berlin tire company. Remarque's lifelong interest in racing cars became intense during this period and gave him the knowledge required to write articles for a Swiss automobile magazine. (These moments found their later expression in his 1961 novel, *Heaven Knows No Favorites*.)

In 1929, Remarque published his first novel, *All Quiet on the Western Front* (the German title is *Im Westen nichts Neues*). It had been rejected by one publisher, and another publisher agreed only reluctantly to print it. The novel is intensely anti-war in sentiment, and this was not a popular attitude in Germany at that time. But the book became an immediate and resounding success, selling more than 1 1/2 million copies in its first year: Germany (800,000), U.S.A. (240,000), France (219,000) and Britain (195,000).

1

The novel caused considerable protest and controversy in Germany. Remarque was criticized for a variety of reasons, ranging from attacks on his loyalty to Germany to an inference that his approach toward war was effeminate.

He refused to declare himself politically or to explain his stand on specific matters of German policy. Rather, his was a novel that exposed war in general, and he had no intention of justifying its contents. He knew that those who attacked his work would probably attack anything that violated their rigid code of values. As a result, he allowed his novel to speak for itself. It has achieved extraordinary success since its publication, having been translated into 25 languages and made into two separate, successful films.

In 1931, Remarque went on to publish a sequel to his first novel. In *The Road Back*, he describes the collapse of Germany in 1918 and the ensuing political disorder in that country. It is no surprise that the German officials resented his books.

In 1932, as the Nazis were growing in power, he left Germany for Switzerland. Despite repeated pleas that he return to his homeland, Remarque stood firm and refused. As a consequence, he was stripped of his German citizenship in 1938. The Germans burned his books and banned his films.

In 1939, he moved to New York and would ultimately become a U.S. citizen (1947). After World War II, he returned to Switzerland with his wife, the actress Paulette Goddard. He published several novels in the post-war period, the most successful of which were *Arch of Triumph* and *Shadows in Paradise*.

Remarque died in 1970, leaving behind *All Quiet on the Western Front*, a novel that has become recognized as the definitive exposé of war.

List of Works

All Quiet on the Western Front	1929
The Road Back	1931
Three Comrades	1937
Flotsam	1941
Arch of Triumph	1946
Spark of Life	1952
A Time to Love and a Time to Die	1954
The Black Obelisk	1957
Heaven Has No Favorites	1961

The Night in Lisbon   1964
Shadows in Paradise (published posthumously
       in English)   1972

Introduction to World War I

World War I, the Great War of 1914-1918, was to be the war that ended all wars. In fewer than three decades, however, Europe would be plunged anew into a war that would claim twice as many lives.

The four long years of WWI remain ever-present as a reminder of the atrocities of war. Ambition, greed, power and confusion were all ingredients in the onset of war. And while it was the assassination of the Archduke Francis Ferdinand in 1914 that formally began the upheaval, we must return to the 19th century to see what conflicts paved the way to this period of violence.

In this Note, we shall look at the major situations and ideas that evolved into WWI and that characterized the 1914-1918 period. Once you understand the general flow of history, your examination of *All Quiet on the Western Front* will take on a deeper, more comprehensive meaning.

The Pre-War Period (1866-1914)

The 19th century had its share of wars, but none of them lasted long, nor were the death tolls extraordinary. These are important facts to keep in mind since Germany, one of the major aggressors in WWI, felt it would win the war profitably in a short period of time. However, the war dragged on much longer than anticipated, due in part to the complexities involved in a multi-national struggle.

The 19th century was the age of the Industrial Revolution. It was a period of growing power, wealth and productivity. Governments believed in progress and in trading with other countries. This gave rise to an interdependence of nations on each other, whereby a people could grow stronger through trade with foreigners.

By the end of the century, Europe was more or less defined clearly into a pattern of nation-states, even if some of these had been formed more recently than others. Despite their interest in trading with other countries, governments also had a desire to expand. For this reason, they scrutinized other nations carefully so as to maintain a healthy political balance of power.

There were four Great Powers: Germany, Russia, Austria and France. Each wanted greater power and wealth. As we examine the highlights of the events leading to WWI, we shall realize that it was the imbalance that evolved among these four nations that ultimately provoked war.

Germany was central to the conflict. In 1866 and 1870, Otto Bismarck's Prussia scored two important victories by uniting Germany into her orbit, destroying the military strength of France and founding the German Empire (the strongest single state in Europe). Bismarck was a shrewd, steady man whose ambitions were not rash or hasty. Though he had made France into an enemy, he was prepared to manipulate political power so that Germany enjoyed the greatest advantage without paying an inappropriate price.

He succeeded in attracting Austria and Italy into an agreement with Germany — called the Triple Alliance — and in originating a "reinsurance treaty" with Russia, stating that Russia was guaranteed against any Austro-German attack.

Short wars had always been profitable for Germany. Young William II, who became the Kaiser in 1888, decided that money could be made by moving the country toward additional wars. This proved to be the most costly error of all times to pre-war Germany, since the Kaiser underestimated the strength of other European nations.

In 1890, the Kaiser dismissed Bismarck, who was not in agreement with these aggressive plans. In 1891, the reinsurance treaty with Russia lapsed and this served to break up the Bismarckian system of strength. The Russian Czar, Nicholas II, had ambitions in the Balkans, as did Austria, so in order to increase Russia's strength, the Czar entered into a pact with France, Germany's mortal enemy. This created the Franco-Russian Alliance of 1895.

The Kaiser, not to be outdone, began developing the German navy — a move that aroused Britain's suspicions. Britain, traditionally considered the ruler of the waters, sought support against a possible German invasion. This led, in 1902, to the Anglo-Japanese Alliance, whereby each country promised assistance to the other in event of a war with more than one opponent. Britain then settled her outstanding disputes with France (1904) and Russia (1907), thereby creating the Triple Entente. This placed Britain right in the middle of the anti-German camp.

Italy, which had been allied with Germany, was no longer indebted to that alliance since there was a secret clause that exempted her from any wars against Britain. Therefore, Italy was no longer on the German side, nor were Britain, France or Russia. This gives us an idea of the mounting tensions and of the two-sided struggle that was about to erupt.

The Crowning Blow: Assassination of Archduke Francis Ferdinand (1914)

The two major storm centers that precipitated the war crisis were Morocco and the Balkans. We will not focus on the complete details of each struggle since this would require volumes. Furthermore, it can be pursued in any competent history book of that period. But we need to mention that both Russia and the Austria-Hungary Power had designs on the Balkans. The Balkans were a group of small kingdoms that had grown stronger in the 19th century as the power of Turkey declined. They comprised Bulgaria, Greece, Serbia and Montenegro, and they sought to inherit whatever Turkish strength remained in Europe.

The Power of Austria-Hungary occupied two Turkish provinces and had ambitions for expansion in that area, even though the Serbs claimed these provinces, Bosnia and Herzegovina, as their own. The conflict, then, was for control of territory; the rivals in the conflict were the Power of Austria-Hungary and the small kingdoms of the Balkans.

The situation was further complicated when Russia announced its desire to protect her Slav kinsmen in Serbia and Bulgaria, with a particular desire to possess Constantinople. At the same time, Morocco was considered to be a satellite of France.

In 1905, Germany saw that Russia was on the verge of a revolution, having just been defeated by Japan. This prevented Russia from being a strong ally to the French, and the Kaiser believed it was an opportune time to possess Morocco. He differed from Bismarck in one important regard: he wanted to spread German control and influence throughout the world, not just Europe. This mammoth ambition is what ultimately brought Germany to her knees.

Early in 1906, Austria was the only power to back Germany at Algeciras. The ten other states assembled at the Conference

5

of the Powers sided with France in the struggle for Morocco. This aggravated the Kaiser and caused resentment, which would spill over into other quests for territory — namely, in the Balkans.

In 1908, the Balkan Crisis occurred, whereby a Turkish revolution detonated a series of events that culminated in World War I. Austria had occupied Turkish provinces under the Treaty of 1878 and, with German backing, moved to annex these provinces without compensating Russia. In conjunction with Russia, Serbia protested this move, since it had wanted to incorporate the Bosnian Serbs living in Turkey. But Russia and Serbia backed down from their protest under threat of war from Austria.

France and Russia saw all this as a danger signal and set about preparing their armed forces. Britain, likewise, understood the growing hostilities and launched a new battleship-construction plan.

By 1911, tensions were high. Italy ignored her obligations to Germany and attacked Turkey in an effort to gain possession of the province of Tripoli. This prompted the four Balkan States to decide that the moment had arrived to divide up the remnants of "Turkey-in-Europe." The First Balkan War of 1912 was a success for the Balkans. But trouble set in when the four states were unable to reach agreement on the division of land. Bulgaria had done most of the fighting and was not prepared to give up what rightfully belonged to her. Therefore, the Second Balkan War of 1913 began, with Bulgaria being defeated by the three other Balkan states, as well as by Rumania.

Germany was delighted at this turn of events. Resentment among the four Balkan countries could prove to be useful to the Great Power. Austria, who still wanted Balkan territory, looked for ways of destroying the now wealthy Serbia. And Germany knew that supporting Austria in the Balkans would be more rewarding than fighting the French in Morocco. All that remained was the necessary stimulus for making a formal declaration of war.

That stimulus arrived shortly. The Archduke Francis Ferdinand, heir to the throne of Austria-Hungary, was sent to Sarajevo, capital of the Serb-populated province of Bosnia. Austria was detested there. On June 28, 1914, Gavrilo Princip, a member of the nationalist Slav terrorists of the Black Hand

Society, fired three shots at the royal car, which contained the Archduke and his wife, Sophie. The couple died within fifteen minutes.

Correlli Barnett, in his excellent book, *The Great War* (London: Octopus Books PLC), pp. 13-15, explains what happened:

> In Vienna the Austrian Chancellor, Count Leopold von Berchtold, and the Chief of the General Staff, Count Franz Conrad von Hötzendorf, were at one in believing that the Archduke's assassination provided the perfect pretext for stopping, once and for all, Serbia's stirring up of Austria-Hungary's South Slav subjects; indeed a final opportunity to restore Austria-Hungary's prestige and halt her slide into disintegration. They wished therefore to force a war on Serbia and smash her. However, behind Serbia stood Russia, self-appointed protector of all Slavs and a long-standing rival of Austria in the Balkans. Before sending Serbia an ultimatum, the Austrian Emperor therefore consulted his powerful ally the German Kaiser. Germany could have held Austria back; instead she gave her the go-ahead. This was partly because the unstable Kaiser was in one of his bellicose moods, partly because German diplomacy felt it could not abandon Germany's only ally. . . .
>
> Europe was divided into two armed camps glowering at each other in mutual fear — the Triple Alliance of Germany, Austria-Hungary and Italy, and the Triple Entente of France, Russia and Britain. . . .
>
> Assured of German backing, Austria-Hungary presented an ultimatum to Serbia on 23 July, giving her 48 hours to accept humiliating terms that would infringe her sovereignty. Nevertheless Serbia returned a submissive answer which the Kaiser himself described as a "capitulation of the most humiliating character." But on 28 July, Austria-Hungary, determined on punishing Serbia, broke off diplomatic relations and ordered part mobilization for a local war against Serbia. Now the crisis had really broken.

Count Berchtold opened the war by storming Belgrade. Most

European officials did their best to avert a general war, but to no avail. Russia, seeing that it would be difficult to travel great distances to the war, began mobilizing herself immediately. With this, Germany declared war on Russia two days later (August 1, 1914).

The War Begins

Since Russia had been declared openly as an enemy by Germany, France had no choice but to support her Russian ally. In an act of arrogance, Germany demanded that the key French fortresses of Toul and Verdun be surrendered to them. This would have crippled her, so France opposed the idea. With this, Germany declared war on France on August 3, 1914 and fighting began in the west.

The following day, Britain declared war against Germany in opposition to Germany's long-planned invasion of Belgium. Turkey, having been stripped of its lands during the Balkan Wars, sided with the Central Powers (i.e., Germany and Austria) but did not enter the action until its October attack on Russia.

Both sides felt the war would be short-lived, and virtually overnight all internal struggles vanished. Countries became quickly unified and defined by the purpose of war. But the British Foreign Minister, Sir Edward Grey, came closer than most to understanding what lay ahead: "The lights are going out all over Europe . . . we shall not see them lit again in our lifetime."

The weapons used were deadlier than imagined and the only reliable way to protect oneself from them was through the entrenchments. Aircraft became increasingly important, despite the large numbers of cavalry.

Battle of the Marne (September 6, 1914)

The Germans were stronger than the other nations. They had more divisions and were better trained. In order to isolate Britain, the Central Powers decided to strike a quick blow against France and barricade Britain from the Continent. Russia provided little threat since her armies were disorganized and run by incompetent men. Germany felt that Russia could be dealt with after France and Britain had been defeated.

Though Belgium was neutral, the Germans saw that their

best entry into France would be through that country. This left only the smallest forces available for protecting the Central Powers from Russia, even though the threat seemed minor.

The British had warned France about the possibility of attack from the north, but the French paid no heed. As Germany entered Belgium, the Belgians refused to tolerate this aggression and fought back valiantly. But they were not strong enough to hold back the Central Powers. On August 23, the town of Namur fell as Germans committed acts of atrocity everywhere they went. This aroused much anti-German feeling among the allies, as well as in North America. The French suffered huge losses in their misguided attempts in the south to drive back the Germans.

It appeared to the Germans as if they had won the war. Britain, France and Belgium had been unable to hold them back, and Russia was not considered a threat. But in their arrogance, they overlooked an important factor: French ingenuity. The right wing of the German army was near Paris and was scheduled to drive the French farther south. But they were unable to surround Paris because of insufficient troops. The French commandant Joseph Gallieni seized the opportunity to strike the Germans in the flank.

Unprepared for this attack, the Germans had left a significant gap between their armies. Into this gap, the French and English launched an attack the next day, thereby initiating the Battle of the Marne. This upset the German plans, and changed the course of the war. Both sides hastened to gain control of the English Channel and the Belgian ports — areas that were crucial to victory.

By November, neither side had made any headway. This was one of the first signs that the war would last a long time. The enemies began fortifying their defences with barbed wire and spades, preparing for a cold winter in the trenches. French and German losses already totalled 854,000 and 677,000 respectively.

Humanity, however, showed itself in an unexpected fashion. On Christmas Day, the British and the Germans struck a truce, which manifested itself in the form of a football match on common ground. This would not be permitted again in the future, since the officials deemed it equivalent to desertion. But it demonstrated the strong desire for peace among the men fighting brutally with each other. Their task was war, but their hearts sought peace. This idea is important to remember when reading *All Quiet on the Western Front*.

Other Developments of 1914

We have already noted that the Russian soldiers were poorly led by incompetent superiors. When Russia attacked Germany from the East, this caused Germany to withdraw some of its troops from France. But since the Russian advance was slow and undisciplined, Germany was able to defend herself under the leadership of Ludendorff. This occurred at the Battle of Tannenberg (August 27-30) and, within a month, three-quarters of the Russian aggressors were killed, wounded or imprisoned.

The vital front of this period was Warsaw, where both sides fought anxiously to control the capital. On December 6, Russia lost the city of Lodz to the west of Warsaw, but, at the same time, the Serbs drove back the Austrians in a last-minute burst of strength.

By the end of 1914, the record shows that Austria had performed ineffectively against the Russians and the Serbs, even though Russia was still on shaky ground. But since the Western Front had become well organized in the trenches, Germany was able to send troops back east to fight against Russia.

The Events of 1915

Germany knew that there was a stalemate on the Western Front and also that Austria would likely collapse if left to fight the Russians by herself. So she planned to hit Russia hard, while maintaining adequate troops on the Western Front. The Allies were committed to defending Russia but saw this as an opportunity to crack through the German defensive on the west. They refused to believe in the strength of this defensive but soon found out that the Germans would not be easily pushed back.

A young Winston Churchill, then first lord of the Admiralty, suggested a plan that held promise but that was opposed by the authorities. Known as the Dardanelles Expedition, Churchill's plan called for the overthrow by the Allies of Constantinople—the only Turkish city with a munitions factory. Turkey was on the German side, and if the Allies could close off this area from the Central Powers, considerable progress toward victory would be possible.

But Britain failed to commit herself thoroughly to this effort, preferring to send troops in fits and starts. The attack began on February 19, 1915 and continued for a month. After a series of surprise attacks by the Turks, Sir Ian Hamilton decided to land the British on the Gallipoli peninsula instead of on the mainland or the Asiatic shore. From April 25 until mid-December, British forces missed one opportunity after another to capture the area.

Finally, the Allies ordered their forces out of the Dardanelles, despite a risk of moral humiliation. This ended a brilliantly conceived plan, which had failed due to abominable execution.

On the Western Front, things had not changed much. The generals believed in the theory of attrition, whereby the war would be won by the side that could survive longer than the other. It is a fact, however, that the Allied method of constant attacks against the German front cost the Allies almost twice as many deaths as the Germans.

There was the added tactic, used by the Germans, of sending chlorine gas in the direction of the Allies. This proved to be an error, however, since the Allies were quick to copy them and could use the gas more ferociously: the wind blew more regularly toward the Germans. Yet the stalemate continued.

The Germans, however, continued their move against Russia. One in three Russian soldiers was unarmed and, by late June, Warsaw was threatened from the south. Germany read the situation correctly and realized that Russia was in despair. She offered the Russians an immediate peace so that the war on the Western Front could be intensified, but the Czar Nicholas refused to negotiate. He preferred to honour his commitment to the Allies.

For that reason, Warsaw fell on August 4 as the Russians retreated quickly from the disaster. Two million Russians had died or been captured, and the Russian prisoners aided the Central Powers by strengthening the labour pool.

The Events of 1916

It was in 1916 that Erich Maria Remarque was drafted into the army, trained and began fighting at the Front. We have seen already how discouraging the situation was on the Western Front, with little progress being made on either side. This atmosphere of frustration and unease will be brilliantly communicated in Remarque's novel. A knowledge of the historical events of this time leads us directly to an understanding of *All Quiet on the Western Front*.

By early 1916, it looked as if the Germans might win. They had done well on the Eastern Front and seemed to be holding their own on the Western Front. But the Allied naval attack grew in strength and threatened to be awesome if the conflict was prolonged. The Germans knew this and realized that victory could only be won on the Western Front. But a series of repeated attacks aimed directly at the front had proven useless to the Allies, so Germany sought other ways of scoring points. Their eventual plan of attack centered on the fortress of Verdun.

Verdun was the major site of the French defence system. It was a salient fortress, which is to say that it projected outward from its foundation and could be attacked on three sides. Heavy bombarding by the Germans could spell death to the French army. On February 21, they had defeated the front line of French soldiers and by the 24th, the second line was eliminated as well. This was in large part due to the erroneous military planning of the French: thinking that their fortresses were not effective, they disarmed them and moved their men into the trenches.

Luckily for the French, they were able to hold on to Verdun and resist the Germans, but only after many last-minute moves to reoccupy the forts. French morale was low, however, and the British had to intervene more heavily.

The British knew that they had to attack the Germans in order to relieve the pressure on the French at Verdun. Given the situation, they decided to renew their attack on the front, particularly in the north were the German defences were strong. This was known as the Offensive on the Somme. The attacks on Verdun had drained the French army, so the British were obliged to assume the lead. The offensive began on July 1, 1916.

The Germans were well organized and in good spirits, compared to the demoralized French and overburdened British. The Allies attacked the Germans with 15 divisions on a front of 15 meters north of the Somme River. They had not concealed their plans, and the Germans were prepared. Consequently, three out of every five Allied soldiers were killed or wounded. On July 1, the British army suffered its greatest losses in one day—60,000 casualties. This is the kind of atrocity that Remarque will expose in his novel from a completely bipartisan, human viewpoint.

The fighting continued into September, with assorted victories being won by the Allies. The tanks were effective against German barbed wire and trenches but moved slowly and had only a short range of attack. By October, rains turned the battlegrounds into vast expanses of mud. This prevented any further fighting. Neither side had won in this offensive, and the war laboured on.

On the Eastern Front, Russia was still not to be forgotten. Her losses had been much less severe than anticipated by the Central Powers, and she was still not ready to surrender to Austria. On June 4, Russia attacked full-scale along the Galician front, taking Austria by surprise and crippling her in the process. In fewer than three weeks, at least 200,000 soldiers had been taken prisoner by the Russians—and many of these men had willingly deserted the Austrian camp.

The Rumanians, in the meantime, had had an excellent opportunity to invade Austria along an unguarded border. But hesitation and disorganization kept them from being effective. Before long, they had lost their capital and three-quarters of their country to the Central Powers. This helped the Germans by making available to them greater supplies of food and oil, but it put added pressure on their Eastern Front efforts since they now had to guard a larger territory.

The principal sea battles took place between Britain and Germany in the North Sea and near the British Isles. In a decisive battle on May 30, 1916, Britain sent six battle cruisers in search of the German ships, apparently headed toward Norway. But Britain was not aware of the German plan, which was to sink the royal ships through submarines and mines. Four of the six British ships were destroyed. Known as the Battle of Jutland, this set-back for the British did nothing to undermine their control of the seas. They remained strong, despite their losses.

The Events of 1917
By early 1917, the United States had not yet entered the war. President Woodrow Wilson sought ways of bringing about peace between the two sides, but his efforts were in vain. When Germany declared herself unwilling to listen to him, symbolized

in the sinking of American ships, Wilson shelved his hesitations and declared war on Germany. This was on April 6, 1917.

Things had not been easy for the Allies. Little had been accomplished at sea or on land, and the stalemate seemed insurmountable. Depression was rampant. The French population had tired of their leader Joseph Joffre and replaced him with the glory-seeking Nivelle. The latter underestimated the weakened state of the French armies and made suggestions that would change the Allies' plan for 1917. The resulting delays cost the Allies precious time and gave Germany the chance to anticipate their actions.

The Allies wanted to renew fighting in the old battleground of the Somme. Predicting this, the Germans quickly fortified the area, creating a new line of defence, which they called the Siegfried and which the Allies called the Hindenburg line.

On April 9, the Allies scored an initial success by taking Vimy Ridge. But they maintained bombardment longer than necessary and, as a result, wasted time and money. French morale quickly succumbed to further depression at the prospects of making no headway on the front.

The French people voted for another switch in leadership, this time replacing Nivelle with Henri Pétain. Pétain's goal of restoring his soldiers' morale placed most of the responsibility for war efforts in the hands of the British. While British manpower was strong on the front, it was not helped by the fact that Russia was doing little to pressure Germany on the Eastern Front.

By July, the British were determined to end the war through prolonged bombardment. On July 31, they launched a major attack at Ypres, in the north of France. Their offensive, however, was weakened by two factors: rain turned the area into a quagmire, and the British disregard for the element of surprise proved to be an oversight. By early November, their attempts at victory were wiped away in the soggy swamps of Passchendaele. It was too wet and too obstructed for battle in Flander's fields.

Matters were not helped by the growing unrest in Russia. The Russian leadership had, for a long time, failed to provide confident, reassuring direction for the Russian people. There were large masses of men ready to fight and there was no shortage of energy or back-up support. But, quite simply, the armies distrusted their leaders and were morally unprepared to rally to their cause.

The Russian Czar had surrounded himself with men whom only he trusted. Riots broke out in March, and he proved unable to cope with them. As a result, his armies sided with the rioters, and he had no choice but to abdicate. Two parties sought to fill the political void: the liberal Provisional Government of Aleksandr Kerensky (which was in favour of war) and the Petrograd Soviet (which opposed war). The Soviet supporters persuaded soldiers to lay down their weapons, and the ensuing desertion was greatly pleasing to the Germans. Indeed, they aided Vladimir Lenin in his return to Russia from Switzerland so that he could assume the leadership of the Petrograd Soviet.

Germany moved toward the Russian capital in November and met with little resistance. After all, the people wanted an end to the war and agreed that this was possible if they complied with the Central Powers. Lenin and his Bolshevik Party were prepared to negotiate. After much discussion, they reached an agreement and signed the Treaty of Brest-Litovsk (March 1918). Through this, Russia was forced to surrender Finland, the Baltic provinces, Poland, the Ukraine and other territories. So while the French and English were fighting vehemently to hold their own in Flanders, the Russians were busy dealing with serious structural problems at home.

Nivelle had been loud about his plans, and the Germans were prepared for him. The result: the French attack was a hopeless failure and brought about countless desertions and mutinies. The soldiers refused to fight the Germans and wanted nothing to do with the frontal offensive. Nivelle was replaced with Pétain. Within three months, Pétain had restored discipline to the army.

A third British attempt to secure the Ypres salient resulted in chaos. The terrain was wet and the tanks would not operate effectively. Human beings dragged themselves through the mud and slime, while morale sank to a new low. In fact, men who fell wounded on the fields of Flanders were marched over by the floundering troops. Conditions were so bad that even the most fleeting of human amenities were trampled into oblivion.

The Events of 1918

By early 1918, it was clear that the Russians would no longer pose a threat to Germany. The Central Powers decided that this was their chance to end the war: they would transfer large numbers of troops to the Western Front and launch an offensive that would destroy the Allies. At this point, it seemed as if the Germans would win the war.

But they realized the need for rapid, decisive movement, since fresh American soldiers were on their way. So they opted for an attack on the British front, judging the British to be very near the breaking-point.

On the morning of March 21, the Germans hit hard and, for the first time, broke through the Western Front. The British and French were thoroughly confused, not knowing where the Germans were coming from or how strong their forces were. But the Germans eventually ceased their advance because of dwindling supplies and difficult geographical conditions. Moreover, their troops needed a pause to recover.

This gave the Allies a chance to strike back. They moved their defences southward in order to meet the German offensive. But by doing this, they weakened their northern line and gave the Germans an additional chance at victory. Erich Ludendorff struck on April 9 in the area between Béthune and Ypres, creating German superiority for nine miles. On April 10, the Central Powers broke through and captured the Messines Ridge.

But the German soldiers became greedy and left their tanks in order to loot the towns. Once morale and discipline were destroyed, the Germans could not afford to continue their forward movement. Their last attempts were on April 29 and, at that point, they called a halt to the offensive.

American troops were arriving in full force and Germany knew time was running out. So Ludendorff made a last-ditch effort to bring about victory. In late May, he moved his armies south toward the Marne River and began an advance toward Paris. But it was too late, thousands of Americans were already on the firing line, and Germany was exhausted.

On July 18, the Allies moved closer to victory. Foch arranged a vital counter-attack against the Germans and had little trouble breaking through. This forced the Germans to begin a withdrawal. On August 8, the Allies attacked them east of

Amiens and forced some of the units to surrender. Ludendorff called this the "black day of the German army."

By the month's end, Germany was moving quickly backward toward the Hindenburg Line but did not have adequate time to rebuild the defences. By the end of September, the Allies had broken the Hindenburg Line. Soon, the German allies began to see the reality of Germany's defeat. They refused to support the Central Powers or risk any more losses. One after another, they fell and surrendered.

Germany continued to retreat along the Western Front but realized the importance of a cease-fire before arriving in German territory. Morale at home was disastrous; everyone knew that Germany had lost the war. On November 9, the Kaiser abdicated, thereby preparing the way for armistice to be signed on November 11.

Peace at Last

The war had been long—much longer than anticipated by either side. Millions of lives had been lost, and the Allies were determined to prevent this from happening again. They knew that the armistice called a halt to the fighting, but that the Germans might wish to take up their guns again at the first opportunity. For this reason, they sought assurances that this would be quite impossible.

According to the armistice terms, Belgium, France, Alsace-Lorraine and Luxembourg were to be evacuated within two weeks. Guns, ammunition and vehicles of transportation were surrendered to the Allies, and Allied prisoners were released from German jails. Along with other restraints on Germany, these items virtually assured the Allies against renewed resistance from the Central Powers.

The terms of peace were worked out primarily by President Wilson, the British Prime Minister, Lloyd George, and his French counterpart Clemenceau. Wilson was instrumental in creating the League of Nations, an organization responsible for preventing all future wars. He also pushed for national self-determination within countries that had hitherto been run by foreign governments. The map of post-WWI Europe was quite different from that of the pre-war days, and Wilson urged that the new states be given power to rule over themselves.

Impact of the War

World War I brought about losses that are too numerous to summarize. Their effects were so widespread that there will never be adequate means of estimating damage.

On the physical level, millions of men were killed. Approximate figures include:

Russia:	1,700,000
Germany:	1,808,545
France:	1,385,300
United Kingdom:	744,702
British Empire:	202,321
Austro-Hungary:	1,200,000
Italy:	460,000
Turkey:	325,000
United States:	115,660

(source: Corelli Barnett, *The Great War*)

Certainly there were greater losses than the above figures reveal, but the tragedy of war makes it impossible to record history in a completely objective manner.

Psychologically, the impact of war was devastating. Men who survived the war carried with them the horrors of physical disgust, emotional revolt, disease, traumas of every sort, memories of rats in the trenches and so on. Their lives had been interrupted by a violent, frustrating conflict which kept them hanging in suspense for years.

The families of the fighters were no less affected. Spouses and children, parents and relatives, friends and lovers were torn apart and assaulted by the uncertainty of loss. No one knew what the next moment would bring, and life as we know it came to a virtual standstill.

No one returns from a war normal. The concept of normalcy becomes an absurd notion, associated with peace-time activities and customary belief systems. War wrenches people from the complacency of day-to-day values and causes them to see things in a profoundly different fashion. God, the country, education, careers, family—all of these take on new meaning to those who have been through war.

Life can never be the same after prolonged stress. The long-term impact of fear, uncertainty, anger and resentment sometimes takes years to overcome. It is not certain, either, that war wounds can be healed—at least on a psychological level. Many men found themselves unable to carry responsibility, to tolerate pressures at work. Large numbers were ill-equipped to assume the ordinary routine of a job, and many were left insecure about everything important to them. The war came as a vast, imposing monster and while sparing many people's lives, nonetheless did irreparable damage to their emotions and bodies.

This is the phenomenon important to Remarque in *All Quiet on the Western Front*. He fought on the Front Line for Germany and despaired over the agonies that this experience brought to his generation.

Introduction to the Novel

No small amount of ink has been poured out on the subject of war. Volumes of theoretical and political arguments offer various modes of interpretation of this highly traumatic human event. Rarely do people agree on the specifics of a particular war, and this serves to prove the underlying feature of human conflict: war occurs when people become sufficiently divided in their beliefs that they begin to fight for superiority and domination.

Most people would agree that war is destructive and disruptive to life. Most people agree that peace is better than war. But the problem sets in when the ways by which people view their homeland differ dramatically from those of opposing parties. Some people are less aggressive than others and prefer to let conflicts go unresolved. They dislike or fear direct confrontation, or they choose to believe that the latter serves to accomplish very little. Others, however, are eager for confrontation. They believe that systems of belief are important and must be defended. They seek to prevent their lives from being influenced by aggressing forces and are prepared to face the necessary evils of war in order to do this.

Whatever we say here must, of necessity, be brief and elementary. The point is war amounts to a show of tactics and force, embodying a measure of luck and good fortune with the ability to sustain an assault to one's strength (money, supplies, manpower, etc.). When reading Remarque's *All Quiet on the Western Front,* it is helpful to know about the events of World War I that caused him to write this novel. And, more importantly, it is essential to ponder one's own reactions to the novel.

Remarque states in a short preface that his book is neither an accusation nor a confession, "and least of all an adventure, for death is not an adventure to those who stand face to face with it." In other words, he has not written his novel in order to titillate, amuse or provoke passive curiosity about his reactions to war. He intends for the reader to be profoundly moved by what he reads—and deeply affected by the atrocities of the war in which Remarque fought. He uses the WWI experiences as a spring-board for the more important issue of war in general and urges the reader to think long and hard about the horrors that such conflicts impose upon the unravelling of civilization.

War is not something that individuals can solve. But collectively we can move toward understanding its causes and avoiding unresolvable disputes. As long as there are people of different languages, religions, cultural beliefs and political ideologies, we are apt to find ourselves in the grips of turmoil. But by becoming more aware of other people's needs and desires, we can perhaps work more closely for universal peace and love. For, in the long run, love can be defined as the unification of the parts into the whole. Regardless of one's personal beliefs, it is difficult to deny that a unified world will be a happier place in which to live.

This is the fundamental message of Erich Maria Remarque's novel *All Quiet on the Western Front*. Peace, serenity, understanding—and *quiet*.

Characters in the Novel

Erna Baumer: Paul Baumer's eldest sister. She is a kind, considerate woman who attends to Paul's needs when he is on leave.

Paul Baumer: The narrator of the novel. 19-year-old Paul is a German soldier on the front line of action. He and his high-school friends have been persuaded to enlist in the army by their schoolmaster, Kantorek.

Josef Behm: A schoolmate of Baumer's. Behm resisted Kantorek's persuasive powers but finally enlisted in the army to avoid being different. A plump, homely boy, he is promptly killed once he joins the army.

Bertinck: The company commander who is killed near the end of the novel. Baumer describes him as ". . . one of those superb front-line officers. . . . "

Detering: A peasant farmer and member of Baumer's unit, who thinks only of his farm and wife. Driven to despair by the war, Detering flees the action and is court-marshalled.

Heinrich Ginger: The cook at the cook-house. Ginger is a bitter man who begrudges the men more than one ration of food.

Corporal Himmelstoss: A contemptible leader of the #9 platoon in which Baumer and his friends serve. Himmelstoss is a strict disciplinarian who carries power beyond its limits. But in the end he redeems himself by befriending the soldiers.

Kantorek: The schoolmaster whose lofty rhetoric about the glory of war entices the young men into the army.

Stanislaus Katczinsky: "Kat" is the leader of Baumer's group of soldiers. He has a knack for finding food when it is scarce. He becomes Baumer's best friend.

Franz Kemmerich: A comrade of Baumer's who is wounded and has his leg amputated. After Kemmerich dies, Baumer must relate the details of the death to the young soldier's mother.

Albert Kropp: A soldier in Baumer's group and a former classmate of Baumer's. Kropp is wounded and suffers great pain in the army hospital.

Leer: A classmate of Baumer's and a soldier in his troop. He has a preference for girls from the officers' brothels.

Mittelstaedt: The schoolmate of Baumer's who avenges the men on Kantorek, their school teacher. He orders Kantorek to perform physically exhausting and demeaning duties.

Müller: A classmate of Baumer's and soldier in his troop. Müller asks for Kemmerich's boots after the latter dies.

Tjaden: A classmate and friend of Baumer's. Tjaden, a skinny, cheerful soul, is nevertheless the biggest eater in the company.

Haie Westhus: Same age as Baumer. He is shot in the back and killed.

Plot Summary

The novel is narrated by Paul Baumer, a 19-year-old German soldier who has fought for his country at the front line. It is written in the style of narrative journal, though at no point does he indicate day-to-day entries.

Paul Baumer and his high-school friends were enticed into the army by the rhetoric of their teacher, Kantorek. He had claimed that fighting for one's country was a lofty, manly way of defining oneself. The men later grew to hate Kantorek and his generation for lying to them. They saw the reality of war and despised everything that it stood for: loss of freedom, loss of family, loss of life.

Their commander, Himmelstoss, is a petty tyrant, loathed by everyone. He is a postman in civilian life and, given some measure of power in the army, abuses his authority in ways that demean the soldiers.

As new soldiers arrive on the front, Baumer and his comrades teach them the necessities of self-protection. Katczinsky, who becomes Baumer's best friend, is an older, wiser man who shows great patience and understanding with the new recruits.

The men plot revenge against Himmelstoss and cause him to re-evaluate his wrongdoings. Through a series of difficult moments at the front, he sees the men's daily traumas and comes to realize what a tyrant he has been. He approaches them for forgiveness, and they accept his friendship.

Action at the front is arduous. Men are killed at every moment and gruesome details are reported. Bodies are blown apart, an entire graveyard explodes into bits, and cadavers in coffins come flying into the air, emptying their wooden boxes for the newly dead. Baumer's troop is held together by brotherhood, love and support. The social facade is gone, leaving only a desire to survive and to return home in peace.

The novel takes us from the earlier period of the war through to the end in 1918. One by one, Baumer's friends are killed: Müller dies; Westhus is shot in the back; Kat is first wounded in the shin, then hit in the head, and so on. At the very end, Baumer, the narrator, is killed on a quiet, uneventful day at the front. Peace is just around the corner, but his life is taken nonetheless. The day was so still on the front that the army report had summed it up in one sentence: "All quiet on the Western Front."

Chapter by Chapter
Summaries and Commentaries

CHAPTER 1

Summary

The novel is narrated in the first person by Paul Baumer, a soldier in the German army fighting on the Western Front. While the novel is not explicitly autobiographical, there is no question that Baumer is a mouthpiece for many of Remarque's experiences during World War I.

The novel opens with Baumer and a group of soldiers at rest, five miles behind the front line. They have been removed from action one day earlier and are now content to be enjoying plentiful meals. They feel more at peace. Baumer's comrades, Tjaden and Müller, produce two wash-basins, and they have all received a double ration of cigarettes.

Baumer explains, however, that this bounty of supplies is the result of an error. Two weeks earlier, they had been summoned up to the front line as a relief team. But there was little action in his sector until the last day, when a great number of English field guns opened fire on them. This reduced the size of the German troop from 150 to 80, thereby leaving more than an adequate stock of food. Still, they have had next to no sleep and have been living under great pressure: " . . . fourteen days is a long time at one stretch."

Baumer agrees with Katczinsky that the war would not be so bad, if only they could get more sleep. This defines his initial position vis-à-vis the war. He is not enthusiastic about it, but nor is he bitter or in despair. At least, not at this point.

Baumer mentions briefly the three other men around him who joined the army as volunteers, as he did. Albert Kropp is the clear thinker who was first to become lance-corporal; Müller is a scholar and fantasizes about examinations as he mutters about physics; Leer has a beard and is interested primarily in girls from the officers' brothels. All four men are 19 years old.

Four other characters are introduced at this point: Tjaden is a skinny locksmith, also 19, who eats more than anyone in the company; Haie Westhus, 19, is a peat-digger [peat is decomposed, partially carbonized vegetable matter used for fuel]; Detering is a peasant who thinks only of his wife and farmyard;

and Stanislaus Katczinsky, the leader of Baumer's group, who is described as being "shrewd, cunning, and hard-bitten, forty years of age, with a face of the soil, blue eyes, bent shoulders, and a remarkable nose for dirty weather, good food, and soft jobs."

It is just past noon, and the group has lined up for food at the cook-house. Katczinsky tells Heinrich, the cook, to begin serving food, but the latter refuses until everyone has arrived. When he discovers that many of the expected men have been killed, the cook's tone changes. He is visibly upset, having cooked for 150 soldiers. Tjaden, interested mostly in food, rejoices at the abundance of prepared bread, sausage and drink.

Heinrich is unwilling to go along with them. While he has food for 150, he will only issue rations for the 80 men present. Katczinsky and the others are angered since, more than once, Heinrich was responsible for their food having arrived cold and late. Baumer explains: "Under shellfire he wouldn't bring his kitchen up near enough, so that our soup-carriers had to go much farther than those of the other companies."

Their lieutenant arrives. As a non-commissioned officer, he has worked his way through the ranks and understands the plight of being a soldier. He sees what is on his men's minds and orders the cook to serve up the entire lot of food.

Baumer is happy about the day's events: The mail has arrived, and almost every man has received a letter. Kropp has received one from their former schoolmaster, Kantorek, who sends his best wishes. The four men who were together in school have mixed reactions about Kantorek. He used to give them long lectures about patriotism, with the result that the whole class decided to volunteer for the army.

Baumer distrusts Kantorek, believing him to have encouraged many men into a situation that is horrifying. Josef Behm was the only schoolboy who had resisted Kantorek's charm. Plump and homely, he later agreed to serve in the army so as not to be ostracized. It was essential not to be considered a "coward"—a term that even the boys' parents were prepared to use of any unwilling children.

In discussing Behm, Paul Baumer confesses that "no one had the vaguest idea" what they were in for when they joined the army. And Behm was one of the first to die. He was hit in the eye during an attack and was left to die on the field. While

Baumer does not blame Kantorek personally for Behm's death, he points the finger generally at the "thousands of Kantoreks" out there who propel men into war. He feels they betrayed him and his friends: "they let us down so badly."

The "Kantoreks" had represented authority. When the young men saw their first death, they lost their faith in this external authority and realized the need to trust their own generation. Their teachers and parents had let them down. War was not glamorous or inspiring. Long gone was the excitement of the Napoleonic period. Baumer sums up these feelings of disenchantment in a key passage:

> For us lads of eighteen they ought to have been mediators and guides to the world of maturity, the world of work, of duty, of culture, of progress—to the future ... in our hearts we trusted them. The idea of authority, which they represented, was associated in our minds with a greater insight and a more humane wisdom. But the first death we saw shattered this belief. We had to recognize that our generation was more to be trusted than theirs. They surpassed us only in phrases and in cleverness. The first bombardment showed us our mistake, and under it the world as they had taught it to us broke in pieces.

Baumer reproaches the older generation for ignoring reality, for pursuing their academic thoughts at the same time as men were being killed. They taught patriotism and duty to one's country, but the soldiers knew the importance and agony of death. This is what disturbs Baumer the most and what causes his friends to laugh at Kantorek's message to Kropp: "Kantorek sends you all his best wishes."

Having experienced the trauma of hypocrisy and hollow values from the authorities' life-style, Baumer and his peers are now alone in the shambles. They know that meaning must be reconstructed and that the way of life can never be the same as it was.

They go to see Kemmerich, who has just had his leg amputated. Müller, who has little tact, prepares to tell Kemmerich about his leg, but Baumer kicks his shin. The man is close to death—this same man who, just a short while ago, was with Baumer and the others, roasting horseflesh by the fire.

Baumer recalls the sentiments of Kemmerich's mother the day she drove her son to the train station. She wept continuously and asked Baumer to look after her son. Now the young soldier lies helplessly in pain, drowsy and unaware of his condition. Baumer knows that he will have to write a letter to Mrs. Kemmerich, and he dreads the idea.

Müller appears with Kemmerich's boots. Since Kemmerich has undergone an amputation and is not likely to survive, the boots are of no further use to him. The men realize that the orderlies will grab them when he dies, so Müller asks permission to keep them. But Kemmerich values his boots and will not part with them.

Finally, they bribe an orderly to give Kemmerich a shot of morphine. In the meantime, Müller remains obsessed with the boots and wonders whether Kemmerich will last until the next day's drill.

Back in their hut, the men react individually to the stresses at hand. Kropp calms down from his anger, after having accused the orderly of looking after the officers at the expense of the soldiers. Then he laughs at Kantorek's comments in his letter; Kantorek had referred to the men as "the Iron Youth." They smirk at the notion of being "youth." Though none of them is older than 20, youth is something that passed them by a long time ago. "We are old folk," says Paul.

Commentary

This first chapter is vital to the structure of the novel. In it, most of the major characters are introduced and the scene is set for an unravelling of a psychological drama. Remarque will vary the tone of each chapter so as to build to a riveting level of tension. The primary purpose of Chapter 1 is to place the story in its context and lay the foundation for the growing turmoil.

As the novel begins, the principal characters are removed from the front-line action. They have been withdrawn after several days at the front and are now in a comparatively relaxed situation. Baumer comments that "We are satisfied and at peace." Of course, this is ironical, given the situation of war. Moreover, Remarque must begin the action at a low point of tension. Otherwise, he would have no chance to develop the chaos of emotions.

So the novel opens "at peace." And, as other novelists

have done, Remarque will bring us full cycle in the story, by concluding the drama with "All quiet on the Western Front." In between this so-called peaceful introduction and quiet conclusion, we have the novel.

Because of the numerous killings, Baumer's troop has been reduced from 150 to 80 soldiers. This sets them up with plenty of food, water, cigarettes and so on. It gives them a boost in morale to realize that, for once, their needs may be provided for. And yet they are on edge: their freedom has been removed, and they are still at the mercy of the army.

While Baumer asserts that war would not be so bad if only they could get more sleep, we hear through his words an attempt to minimize the pain. Very few people enjoy the act of war, and sleep is probably the best defence mechanism for shutting this out. Baumer is saying, in effect, that he would rather substitute freedom and peace for the agonies of battle.

And he is not alone in this attempt. Death is a hard reality confronting each of them. They witness the mutilation of friends and loved ones as they fight what seems to be an endless, futile struggle. Katczinsky, whom they call Kat, makes light of their trauma when he explains to Heinrich, the cook, that some of the men will be absent from dinner since they're "pushing up daisies." As with many doctors who, on the surface, take death in an apparently detached, unemotional manner, the soldiers must reduce their personal pain by whatever means they can.

The matter of patriotism and glory is brought to the fore in this chapter. Baumer's schoolmate, Josef Behm, had been the only one to refuse co-operation with the army efforts. He had not wanted to enlist, nor had he been snared by the rhetoric of his teachers. But the pressures of being an individual, of standing out from the crowd, were more than he could take. Rather than daring to remain alone, he succumbed to their requests and signed up for the war.

Behm was one of the first to be killed. This is Remarque's way of showing the war rolls over even the most individualistic of men. It cares nothing for personal preference or commitment to ideals. War is war. Behm might well have been alive after the war if he had stuck to his principles. But the attitude of others toward him caused him to follow the crowd.

Behm was idealistic in the sense that he saw for himself a better world than that of war. But he was also realistic, realizing that war would surely not be the place for him. He was correct. The others had been led on by their teacher, Kantorek, whose dynamism about the war prompted them to enlist without questioning their motives.

Kantorek and his generation were the authorities. They represented for Baumer and his peers a group of human beings worthy of trust, capable of sound judgment. The Kantoreks of the world spoke not from wisdom or experience, but from lofty romanticism and arrogance about their country. They thought of supremacy and power rather than individual hardship and family tragedy. In short, they acted selfishly and unknowledgeably, without regard for human dignity or suffering.

But the young soldiers only understood this after seeing death at their feet. Kantorek's long lectures on patriotism held no water after this. Yet it was too late to turn back. Their world was now changed, and they had to reconstruct for themselves what they could from the ashes of torment.

In *The Catcher in the Rye*, the narrator, Holden Caulfield, decides that his purpose in life is to protect young people from the vulgarities of the world. He chooses to be a "catcher" in a field of "rye" so that he is able to catch innocent children before they fall over the cliff into the gulf of wicked adulthood. This is the kind of person, according to Baumer, that Kantorek and his colleagues ought to have been for the youth of Germany: "For us lads of eighteen they ought to have been mediators and guides to the world of maturity. . . . "

This rupture from civilization has left the soldiers with no roots and no stability. They are torn from their families and stripped of their identities. One dare not be an individual in the army; one must be subordinate to the group. One fights for the nation, not for the self, regardless of personal conviction.

As a result of this severance from a structured society, the men are at odds with themselves. Their idealism about war is destroyed, and the only path left to them is that of intense realism. They understand their plight, despise their state of slavery, and wish only for peace. In a moment of obsession for material stability, Müller determines to seize Kemmerich's boots when the man dies. The boots, while perhaps more comfortable than his present ones, represent Müller's need for structure. They are a focal point around which he can center his energies and through which he can construct a more complete world for himself. It is important, for one who has lost everything, to accumulate objects of value.

We should recall that Remarque fought in this war and has colourful memories of its events. The intensity of Müller's desire and of Baumer's sorrow over Kemmerich are emotions anchored in reality. That is what makes this novel a truly great exposé of war.

CHAPTER 2

Summary

Baumer resumes his narration with a reminiscence about his unfinished play, *Saul*, which lies in a drawer at home along with a bundle of poems. But this remains a part of his life that no longer means anything to him. The war has separated him from the luxury of creation. "Our early life [i.e. their pre-army days] is cut off from the moment we came here. . . . We often try to look back on it and to find an explanation, but never quite succeed. For us young men of twenty everything is extraordinarily vague. . . . "

The older men have wives, families, jobs, etc., but the younger soldiers have practically nothing. They have not had the chance to establish themselves in life, and the war has robbed them of this opportunity. "We young men of twenty, however, have only our parents, and some, perhaps, a girl—that is not much, for at our age the influence of parents is at its weakest and girls have not yet got a hold over us."

Kantorek would have said that they stood on the threshold of their lives. Although Baumer believes that the war has swept them away, they are not sad. It is a fact of life that they have accepted, even if with resentment.

Müller still waits for the moment when he can seize Kemmerich's boots. It is not that Müller is an insensitive or vicious man. Müller knows that the boots will be of no use to a dead man. And he feels that he can make better use of them than the orderlies.

Baumer explains the situation concerning the boots. "We have lost all sense of other considerations, because they are artificial. Only the facts are real and important for us. And good boots are scarce." In other words, Müller is not being petty or tactless—merely realistic.

Describing the ins and outs of war, Baumer points out the adjustments that they endured immediately after signing up for training. Filled with the romantic and idealistic notions of Kantorek and his generation, the young men quickly realized that the boot brush was more important than the mind and that the system counted more than intelligence.

We became soldiers with eagerness and enthusiasm, but they have done everything to knock that out of us. After three weeks it was no longer incomprehensible to us that a braided postman should have more authority over us than had formerly our parents, our teachers, and the whole gamut of culture from Plato to Goethe.

This amounted to an abandonment of individual personality: soldiers were compelled to give up their uniqueness and mold themselves into a unified block.

When they arrived in the army, Baumer, Kemmerich, Kropp and Müller were assigned to the ninth platoon, under the supervision of Corporal Himmelstoss. The corporal was a strict disciplinarian and proud of it. In civilian life, he was a postman, and he especially disliked several of the men (including Baumer, Kropp and Tjaden) because he sensed quiet defiance in them.

Himmelstoss is the typical boorish army officer who uses his special power to inflict pain on subordinants. As a civilian, he would have had no superiority over these men, but by virtue of his position in the army, he was able to make them suffer for minor, petty reasons. For example, he made Baumer remake his bed fourteen times one morning.

Himmelstoss is sadistic. He creates difficult situations for his men and takes pleasure in seeing their helplessness. Once, however, he made Baumer and Kropp clear the barrack-square of snow with a hand-broom and a dust-pan. A lieutenant accidentally came by, saw them, and severely criticized Himmelstoss for his insolence. This, of course, made Himmelstoss hate them even more and caused him to subject them to further indecencies.

Himmelstoss was eventually put in his place, and by the very men whom he had mistreated. One day, Baumer was at bayonet practice with him and was made to use a heavy iron weapon, while Himmelstoss pranced about with a light wooden one. This inequity caused Baumer's arm to bruise rapidly as Himmelstoss struck him relentlessly. In fury, Baumer ran at him and jabbed him in the stomach, knocking him down.

When Himmelstoss reported the incident to his superior, the latter was delighted at Himmelstoss' discomfort. He understood Himmelstoss' depraved behaviour and was pleased to see him suffer at the hands of his men. Later, the soldiers continued to take orders from him, but they did so with slowness and irony. An order was an order, but they knew they had defeated him.

Reflecting on these early army experiences, Baumer states that they toughened people up. "We became hard, suspicious, pitiless, vicious, tough—and that was good; for these attributes were just what we lacked." It was good preparation for them before entering the trenches; otherwise, they would have gone mad.

The one remarkable thing that grows out of this sordid experience is the *esprit de corps* (regard for honour) among the men. It is a strong, practical bond, "which in the field developed into the finest thing that arose out of the war—comradeship." The knowledge that they are not alone in their suffering and unhappiness, that others share it with them, brings the men together into a cohesive support group. It is the thread of humanity necessary for survival.

Baumer and Kemmerich have a conversation. Kemmerich is too ill to be moved but knows about his amputated leg. Baumer assures him that he will soon go home, and Kemmerich asks him repeatedly if this is true.

Kemmerich lapses into silence, then announces that he once wanted to be a head-forester. Baumer tries to arouse optimism and life in him by reinforcing the idea of getting better. But it is in vain. Kemmerich informs Baumer that he may take the boots to Müller—a symbolic gesture that prepares us for his death.

Baumer takes a long look at his friend, realizing that the end is near. Kemmerich's skeleton has begun to work its way through the flesh, and his skin has become very pale. While trying to remain optimistic, Baumer knows that this is his friend in pain.

In a whisper, Kemmerich requests Baumer to send his watch home if it is found. Someone had stolen it from him earlier, and the men knew this would also happen to his boots if some provision were not made in advance. Baumer feels wretched with helplessness.

Kemmerich begins to cry, softly and without energy. An orderly passes by impatiently to see if he is dead; evidently he wishes to have the bed. For an hour, Baumer sits closely, waiting to help his friend if possible. As Franz begins to gurgle, Baumer yells for the doctor, who in turn sends the orderly in his place. The doctor is described as being short-tempered and dispassionate about the notion of death. He has already amputated five legs in one day. Already sixteen men have died this day; Kemmerich will be the seventeenth. They expect twenty.

When they arrive at Kemmerich's bed, he is dead. His face is still wet from the tears. They move Franz onto a waterproof sheet and prepare the bed for another wounded man.

Baumer makes his way outside where the wind blows in his face. "Thoughts of girls, of flowery meadows, of white clouds suddenly come into my head. My feet begin to move forward in my boots, I go quicker, I run. . . . I breathe the air deeply. The night lives, I live. I feel a hunger, greater than comes from the belly alone."

He arrives at the hut and gives the boots to Müller.

Commentary

There are two primary divisions in this chapter: on the one hand, it is an explanation of the traumas suffered during Baumer's early days in the army; on the other, it describes the agonizing final moments in the life of Kemmerich.

The chapter begins metaphorically. The author-narrator discusses the act of writing his play and poetry. But he acknowledges that such flights into fantasy are too unreal for the moment; war is the major event on their minds. So we have the author, Remarque, writing about writing, and the narrator, Baumer, concluding that fiction must be shelved until reality has been dealt with. It is one way for Remarque to assert that the story we are reading is inspired by reality; it is not fiction or a cooked-up fantasy which belongs "at home in the drawer of my writing table."

This metaphor on writing is a feature of many great literary works. Marcel Proust, Victor Hugo, Charles Dickens and

William Shakespeare all develop it. What interests writers most is the act of writing; it is their means of communication with the world and a medium through which to experiment with ideas. The most effective way for Remarque to present his ideas on war was, obviously, to write about them. Hence, his preoccupation with the process of writing.

The significance of the section devoted to Himmelstoss and the boot-camp days is this: through a series of humiliating activities, Baumer and his friends endured villainies and injustice as never before. Himmelstoss was the representative, in the army, of the authority figures in civilian life—the Kantoreks of their new world. He expected obedience and respect from the men regardless of his requests. As with many minor officers, he gratified himself at the expense of inferiors within the army organization.

But the outrage and frustration of the men led them to restore a balance to this situation. They came to realize that while Himmelstoss' orders must be obeyed, they could do so on their own terms. Shout as he might, there was nothing he could do to speed them up or shake them down. Once they understood that his authority could be destroyed—principally because it was an ingenuine authority in the first place—they rejoiced in their new superiority. And, what's more, Himmelstoss was helpless against them.

This idea of authority struggles has curious implications. It shows that power is a commodity that must be handled deftly and only by those capable of using it for the good of mankind. Power, in the wrong hands, causes pain and suffering. It becomes the tool of the ruthless and the toy of the cruel. The most astounding example of this in recent history is that of Adolf Hitler: power, in his corner, opened the doors to murder of the worst possible kind.

So the Himmelstosses of the German army—or any army, for that matter—create a situation where men fight against each other within the confines of their own organization. It makes for a pressure-builder in an already tense, anxious arena, and it assaults company morale perhaps more wretchedly than anything else.

Power, in an evolutionary system, generally lands in the lap of people sufficiently evolved to understand its implications. This does not mean that they use it correctly. But it is not usually possible for them to have power unless they have been elected democratically or have been appointed through merit. Money, too, plays a role—indeed significantly—in the inheritance or acquisition of power.

But the point is, within the natural system of society, free from the demands of war, power functions almost exclusively in a controlled, scrutinized manner. The free-for-all of war brings about a chaos and confusion, whereby men of all capabilities find themselves in positions for which they are not adequately suited. Such is the case with Himmelstoss. The acquisition of power is such a novelty and source of pleasure to him that he exercises his newly acquired strength in a sadistic, reckless fashion. He is somewhat like a child with a new toy, except that in his case, he prefers smashing and destroying the toy instead of being kind to it.

Justice is done, however, since Himmelstoss is ultimately subjected to the same abuse from his soldiers. The difference is this: whereas he had caused them both physical and mental turmoil, they reciprocated only with a psychological revenge. On the surface, they respected him. But underneath, everyone knew what was happening.

This ties into a much larger system of justice ruled by certain basic laws of the universe. There are rules that govern the development of our lives and that we can manipulate for our own good. Religious groups have known this for generations but refer to it in different ways, depending on the religion. The language of Western religions often refers to "good" and "evil," and in Eastern religions the term "karma" plays a central role.

Here is the key issue: there is a fundamental cosmic law that governs the "good" and "bad" that happens to us. Loosely worded, it goes something like: "What you give is what you get." The *Bible* suggests that we receive ten times in return what we give to others, whether this be money, good deeds, evil acts etc. The Eastern concept of karma is based on the same idea—when we do good, we automatically cause good to be redirected toward ourselves. Likewise, we attract trauma, problems, difficulties and turmoil when we act negatively or with evil intent.

Therefore, it is quite possible to determine one's future—indeed, one's present—by directing energy, thoughts

37

and actions in either a positive or negative fashion. The results of our actions are determined by the actions themselves. In the case of Himmelstoss, we can see clearly what is at stake. He behaves in a harsh, despicable manner and, as a consequence, becomes the victim of his own negativity. The men have no respect for him, they treat him contemptuously, and "it was the end of his authority."

The concept of karma or cause/effect will remain important throughout the entire novel. When we witness negative or "evil" forces at work, we can anticipate negative or "evil" consequences to the person who has originated them. It is a boomerang effect and is central to all moments of human existence. Using this as a tool for understanding human behaviour, you might examine the results of negative or positive actions in your own life. See whether the behaviour of a Himmelstoss doesn't always attract to that person the anger and contempt of his/her peers.

So, by rejecting the authority of Himmelstoss, the soldiers were fulfilling a symbolic catharsis. They were ridding themselves of the numerous authority figures in their pre-war lives and declaring themselves independent of such perverted behaviour. They had been brainwashed and manipulated by their mentors, and now they sought freedom and dignity.

In the second section of this chapter, there is a moving scene between Kemmerich and Baumer. We know that death looms on the horizon for the young Franz. What matters in this scene is the impact of death on the mind of Baumer—his thoughts, feelings and reactions to the experience. Kemmerich had wanted to be a forester, but now this is impossible. His hopes and dreams have been shattered by the war. In fact, his very life has been destroyed.

For Baumer, life is an ambiguous event at this point. Beside the death bed, his concern lies in the assurance of proper care for his friend. He is outraged by the callous behaviour of the orderlies and physicians and realizes that the giant mechanism of war bulldozes over the strongest of human beings. Desire and ambition count for nothing in this death ward. The only link to life is the endless wait, the ticking of time.

When Kemmerich dies, Baumer flees the death scene for a good reason. He is caught in that fragile zone between life and death and knows that a bold proclamation of life is the way to avoid insanity. For this reason, "Thoughts of girls, of flowery meadows, of white clouds" suddenly come into his head. A lack of sensitivity? On the contrary: he is so sensitive that he must saturate himself with the very essence of life, the texture of things human.

Seeing his friend Franz die is the closest Baumer has come to death—other than the more routine exposure to anonymous deaths on the front line. In order to survive, he must redirect his thinking to life and commit himself to the world around him. This is what he means at the end of the chapter when he records: "I breathe the air deeply. The night lives [i.e. *I* am alive] . . . . I feel a hunger, greater than comes from the belly alone." This hunger, of course, can mean many things—not the least of which is his hunger for life, peace, love and tranquillity. He longs for things to be quiet on the Western Front.

CHAPTER 3

Summary

Reinforcements have arrived and the vacancies are filled. Many of the new men are two years younger than Baumer and his friends.

Kat asks one of the new men about the day's meals. The boy grimaces because every meal has been made out of turnips. So Kat takes him over to a tub containing a stew of beef and beans. The youngster has his mess-tin filled, and Kat suggests: " 'Next time you come with your mess-tin have a cigar or a chew of tobacco in your other hand. Get me?' "

Kat is capable of finding food at all times, even when it is scarce. And Haie Westhus is effective as the executive arm operating under Kat's orders.

For instance, one night they land in an unknown spot that has no food, provisions or beds. An artilleryman claims that there is no food to be had, but Kat goes out and returns with fresh bread, horseflesh and a chunk of fat. Baumer thinks that Kat is capable of producing a supper of roast meat, dates and wine while in the middle of a desert.

The first reference to Germany's position in the war comes in this chapter. Tjaden failed to salute a major, so the group of them were ordered to practise saluting all day. Kat comments: " '. . . we are losing the war because we can salute too well.' "

In other words, he believes that the officers are more concerned with decorum and formal behaviour than with winning the war. Germany, at this point, has begun to lose ground.

Kat and Kropp have an argument. Kat's philosophy on the war is: "*Give 'em all the same grub and all the same pay. And the war would be over and done in a day.*" Kropp would like to see war staged like a bull fight, with entrance tickets and bands. The officers and generals of the warring countries would fight it out in the arena, and whoever survived, would win the war for his country.

Sitting in the wretched barracks, they mention briefly their desire to return home, to take up their former lives of happiness and contentment. But they dare not pursue this line of thinking, so the subject changes. They discuss drill. Then they talk about Himmelstoss.

Kat enters into a philosophical explanation of power and Himmelstoss' abuse of authority: " 'In himself man is essentially a beast . . . . The army is based on that; one man must always have power over the other. The mischief is merely that each one has much too much power.' " The more insignificant a man is in civilian life, Kat claims, the more corruptly he uses power in the army.

Kat does not object to discipline. Rather, it is the abuse of power that disturbs him. Kat is amazed that the ordinary soldier survives as long as he does on the front line. The soldiers believe that they know everything they need to know before they get to the line. This attitude comes from their boot-camp training.

Tjaden rushes in, red-faced, to announce the arrival of Himmelstoss. The two men dislike each other. When still in the barracks, Tjaden wet his bed at night and Himmelstoss argued that it was sheer laziness that made him do so. Himmelstoss solved the problem—he thought—by putting another bed-wetter in the bunk above Tjaden. Then, the next night, the two men were to switch beds, thereby establishing a system of retaliation. But it failed to work since neither man wet his bed for reasons of laziness. It was a physical problem over which they had little control. Stress, of course, only made it worse.

Baumer reminisces about the finest day of his army life—the day he spent with Haie just before they left for the front line. They were due to leave early the next morning and, in the evening, prepared to square accounts with Himmelstoss.

They knew which pub he frequented in the evening and that he had to go along a dark road on his way back to the barracks. Baumer, Kropp, Tjaden and Westhus collaborated on an ingenious plan for getting revenge on Himmelstoss. They waited behind a pile of stones and, when Himmelstoss walked past them alone, the men threw a bed-cover over his head from behind. They incapacitated him so that he was unable to raise his arms.

Westhus landed a blow to Himmelstoss' head with his hand working like a coal shovel. When Himmelstoss started yelling, they squelched his noise with a cushion. Tjaden unbuttoned the man's braces and pulled down his trousers. Then began the whipping, and each of them had his turn.

Then Haie Westhus stood him up and gave him another punch. "Himmelstoss yelled and made off on all fours. His striped postman's backside gleamed in the moonlight."

The men disappeared at full speed, and Himmelstoss never discovered who they were.

Commentary

This chapter comes as a relief after Chapter 2, where death and hardship are the focal points. Here, the subject is primarily that of authority and survival.

Kat is shown to be a real survivor. He can find whatever he needs, despite the odds against him. He is a pleasant man, wise in his knowledge of human nature, and he puts into theoretical terms the explanation of power that we have seen described earlier in the novel. He knows that men are essentially animalistic and that they hide this aggression under a facade of social courtesy. But given the chance to snap at power, they do so and often abuse it.

Kat's explanation of misguided authority sets the scene for an enjoyable narrative of the soldiers' revenge on Himmelstoss. In the commentary on Chapter Two, we mentioned the Eastern notion of karma, whereby a certain cause is destined to produce a certain effect. Nowhere is this more colourfully illustrated than in the retaliation against Himmelstoss. Baumer sums up this philosophy of karma as it applies to the present situation: "Himmelstoss ought to have been pleased; his saying that we should each educate one another had borne fruit for himself.

We had become successful students of his method." Evil begets evil, and good brings about good.

The purpose of this chapter, then, is to demonstrate the power of human determination. When it is improperly focused, it can bring about pain and suffering. When guided positively in an organized fashion, it can induce progress of the most fulfilling nature.

CHAPTER 4

Summary

The men prepare for wiring fatigue [a non-military duty] by jamming into the trucks shoulder to shoulder. The weather is warm and everyone is in a good mood. Baumer notes that ". . . we feel drawn together."

They must keep their lights out so as not to be seen by the Allied forces. They hear some geese and decide to capture them later for food.

They arrive at the artillery lines, acrid with the smoke of guns and the fumes of powder. This is the area of the reserves, not the front line. Yet everyone knows that danger is nearby. The sounds of shelling indicate that the English have begun their assault sooner than expected. The men anticipate a bombardment.

Baumer explains that the men's faces are changed by the experience of the front. It is not fear, but rather a thick-skinned attitude of tense waiting. "The body with one bound is in full readiness." It is the earth that befriends soldiers, offering them security and intimate contact in their hours of need.

Upon arrival at a forest, the men climb out of the trucks. They will spend the night in the wood and return in the morning. Troops can be seen marching along the road, with helmets gleaming softly in the moonlight. Gradually, the individuals disappear in the distance, until they are no longer recognizable.

They set out on their mission, which is to lay down wire across the ground. It is a thankless seamy task where flesh can be torn and limbs broken. Everything must be carried out in the dark since they are so close to the line.

As the front line opens up to them, they see a sky aflame with gun fire, "silver and red spheres which explode and rain down in showers of red, white, and green stars." It is a bombardment.

They position the barbed wire at regular intervals, with two men holding a roll of wire, while the others spool it off onto the iron stakes. Baumer completes the job and tries to sleep, but the sea air is too chilly. From this reference to the sea, we can deduce that they are located in the northern France section of the front, or perhaps in Flanders. There are no specific details.

Eventually Baumer falls asleep but is awakened by a nose-cap that has landed in the bushes close to him. Kat is seated within talking distance and comments on the beauty of the fireworks—if only they weren't so dangerous. He is reassuring to Baumer, who appreciates his experienced, wise manner.

Soon the Allied forces attack more strongly, and soldiers run everywhere to escape harm. Baumer comforts a frightened recruit by holding him close to his chest. The fighting eases off temporarily.

In the distance, they hear the sound of wounded horses moaning. Detering prays that someone will put them out of their agony, but Kat responds that the ammunition must first be used on the enemy. It is a scene of horror and ugliness.

As the men make their way back to the spot where the trucks are to pick them up, major gun-fire breaks out. "We duck down—a cloud of flame shoots up a hundred yards ahead of us . . . part of the wood rises slowly in the air, three or four trees sail up and then crash to pieces."

Ironically, the only place to hide is the graveyard. Moments later, the Allies launch such a widespread attack that "The flames of the explosions light up the graveyard." There is nowhere to go. No escape. Baumer feels himself hit by a splinter. Then he is cracked on the skull and begins to lose consciousness.

He quickly searches for cover and avoids losing consciousness by keeping mentally active. Things happen fast and luck plays a major role in survival. It is a gruesome scene, rife with dead bodies and slimy mud. He forces his way toward a coffin and comes face to face with Kat, who screams to him " 'Gas' ", " 'Pass it on.' "

They struggle to put on their gas masks as the explosives drown out all verbal communication among the soldiers. Then a second bombardment begins. "It is no longer as though shells roared; it is the earth itself raging."

Baumer feels pressure building up inside his head. The gas mask can only circulate "the same hot, used-up air." He is close to suffocation.

Having helped a wounded man to splint his arm, Baumer and the others carry him away once the shelling stops. It is daylight now and the graveyard is a "mass of wreckage." They discover a young recruit who has been seriously wounded and will never walk again. It is the one who, earlier, clutched onto Baumer for comfort.

Kat and Baumer know that the youngster will not survive and that his present numbness is better than the days of agony he will suffer if they get him to the first-aid center. They discuss shooting him so that he will be spared further misery, but it is too late: a group of people has gathered around him, so they go get a stretcher.

There are fewer losses than expected: five killed and eight wounded. Baumer and the others return to the trucks. There is more room now than before, and it begins to rain. Everything is monotonous and dull.

Commentary

This chapter comes as a violent shock after the calmness of Chapter 3. In it, we are thrown into a horrifying, bloody bombardment. The author's fine description and attention to detail leaves no emotion unturned. Ultimately, we come away from the chapter with the taste of death in our system, the feeling that war is the epitome of all human tragedies.

At the start, we are led to the front line by Baumer and his peers as they prepare to construct wire fences and barriers. There is a growing fraternity among the men (". . . we feel drawn together"), which gives them strength when they desperately need it. Being alone is never easy, but it is even less so when at war. The comfort of fellow human beings is often the only solace of the moment.

The threat of death at the front line is real. All vanity and social facades are stripped away, and what remains is the most primitive, basic self. Human beings experience a surge of animal impulse as they immediately prepare for the defence against death:

. . . we start out for the front plain soldiers, either

cheerful or gloomy: then come the first gun-emplacements and every word of our speech has a new ring .... We reach the zone where the front begins and become on the instant human animals.

Like animals, the men seek protection on the earth. They crawl, creep and hug the ground under them in an effort to go unseen by the enemy.

Remarque alludes to a fascinating component of the human mind in this chapter. Referring to the instant threat associated with the sound of gun-fire, he indicates the importance of the unconscious mind in protecting oneself from danger. The conscious mind processes information in a systematic, reasoned and organized fashion. This can be time-consuming and tedious when an emergency strikes.

In its place, the unconscious mind can take over and relay important information in fractions of a second. An individual's unconscious mind can be seen as being connected with all other unconscious minds in the world/universe—a phenomenon that the psychologist Carl Jung called the "collective unconscious." It works this way: the human spirit occupies a body but, at the same time, can be in communication with a spirit somewhere else in the world. The communication is non-verbal and immediate. Sometimes we hear of people who experience a hunch or premonition about some event. When they discover later that this "hunch" proved to be accurate, they are often baffled. Much research remains to be done, of course, in the domain of mind power and states of consciousness. But it is helpful to know something about this when reading this passage from Chapter 4:

At the sound of the first droning of the shells we rush back, in one part of our being, a thousand years. By the animal instinct that is awakened in us we are led and protected. It is not conscious; it is far quicker, much more sure, less fallible, than consciousness. One cannot explain it. A man is walking along without thought or heed;—suddenly he throws himself down on the ground and a storm of fragments flies harmlessly over him;—yet he cannot remember either to have heard the shell coming or to have thought of flinging himself down. But had he not abandoned himself to the impulse he would now be a heap of mangled flesh. It is this other, this second sight in us, that has thrown us to the ground and saved us, without our knowing how.

We do not "know how," as it were, because we have no active or conscious recollection of the processes involved. We often know something to be true but cannot prove it. Such is the case with reincarnation, a concept to which Remarque refers in the above selection ("we rush back. . . a thousand years"). Again, the notion of reincarnating in a series of lives is something that troubles or alienates many people. Some biologists might insist that it is merely a genetic echo embedded into our DNA, the genetic code.

But whether Remarque offers this phenomenon of rushing back a thousand years as an example of genetic transmission or reincarnation—or, perhaps, as both—the important point here is that the soldiers under threat respond in a way quite different from normal. Their conscious minds might order them to do one thing, whereas their unconscious instincts thrust them in another direction. Of the two types of mind power, the unconscious holds the greater influence.

The loss of individuality is underlined in this chapter when we see the soldiers marching off into the distance as a block.

Farther on the mist ends. Here the heads become figures; coats, trousers, and boots appear out of the mist as from a milky pool. They become a column. The column marches on, straight ahead, the figures resolve themselves into a block, individuals are no longer recognizable. . . .

Given this loss of individuality, it is no wonder the soldiers feel a strong bond of comradeship with their fellow fighters. And it is further understandable that they would deeply resent the Himmelstosses of the army when they are transferred from the front to the rear.

It is symbolic that, when at war, the men have nowhere to go. They cannot escape their situation unless through death or serious injury. Later, in the aftermath of World War II, the

French writer Albert Camus will use this very sense of isolation to show how alone and lonely human beings are—and how important it is to bond oneself with the mass of humanity. In this context, one often sees critical essays on the "humanism" of Albert Camus and, with Jean-Paul Sartre, the idea of existentialism being humanism. Human beings at war with other human beings can, ironically enough, only seek strength in their love of humanity.

Chapter 4 is a brilliant exposé of war's ugly atrocities. It is an unsettling, provocative chapter in which no details are spared. For once, we see war for what it truly is: a barbaric, crucifying murder of innocent human beings. The lofty and romantic fantasies from the Napoleonic era are dispelled when one realizes that ripped-off limbs and exploded heads are typical, run-of-the-mill consequences of ambitious warfare.

CHAPTER 5

Summary

After a brief passage on their method for killing lice, Baumer reveals that Himmelstoss has arrived at the front line. "He seems to have overdone it with a couple of young recruits on the ploughed field at home and unknown to him the son of the local magistrate was watching. That cooked his goose."

The men recall with great satisfaction the night they thrashed Himmelstoss. Then they discuss what they would do if it were peace-time again. Haie Westhus would stay with the Prussians and serve out his time in the army. The others are aghast at this thinking, but he explains that the army is actually a straightforward, adequate life. It is better than peat-digging. There is food, a bed, clean underwear, a good suit of clothes and evenings in the pub.

Tjaden has only one thing on his mind: to see to it that Himmelstoss doesn't get past him. Revenge, on a daily basis, is his goal.

Detering would carry on with the harvesting. He is worried about his wife, who now has full responsibility for running the farm. It is too much for one woman to handle.

Himmelstoss enters the room, slightly hesitant and with a slow gait. No one says anything to him or attempts to stand up, so he barks: " 'Well!' " He is not sure what to do when the men continue to ignore him. He would like to give them orders, but realizes that the front line is no picnic. Nor is it a parade-ground.

Tjaden lunges forth at him with an insult that makes Himmelstoss boil: " 'Wouldn't you like to know what you are? A dirty hound, that's what you are. I've been wanting to tell you that for a long time.' " Himmelstoss orders him to his feet, but Tjaden tells him to take a run and jump at himself. Himmelstoss orders again, but Tjaden merely "ventilates his backside" at him.

Himmelstoss stomps off, vowing to have Tjaden court-martialled. The men burst into laughter, delighted at the put-down.

But Kat is worried. " 'If he reports you, it'll be pretty serious.' " Tjaden hasn't the remotest fear. If he is sent to the Fortress for five or six days, so much the better. It means that he will be out of action and probably out of danger.

They reminisce about the uselessness of their high-school education. " 'How can a man take all that stuff seriously when he's been out here?' " But Müller insists they must have an occupation. Kropp replies that Kat, Detering and Haie can return to their former jobs, yet the rest of them will be left stranded. They have not completed their education, nor have they been trained for a job. They are in limbo.

Baumer is nauseated by the discussion. Professions and studies and salaries have always disgusted him, and there seems little reason at this point to think about them. The drumming of the war makes such thoughts absurd.

The men feel confused and hopeless. Kropp exclaims: " 'The war has ruined us for everything.' " Baumer adds that they were plucked from life just as they were beginning to find themselves, to enjoy living. Now they are cut off from striving, from progress. Their only belief is in the war.

Himmelstoss returns with the fat sergeant-major, demanding that Tjaden report to him in ten minutes. But Baumer tips Tjaden off, and the latter disappears. Thirty minutes later, Himmelstoss reappears but nobody pays any attention to him. They are playing cards.

That evening, the bunch of them are called into a trial. One after another they testify. Baumer tells Bertinck, the lieutenant, the story about Himmelstoss' solution to the bed-wetting situation. Himmelstoss is called in by the Lieutenant and asked for an explanation. He is obliged to confess.

Bertinck wonders why no one reported this. But no one answers him, since they all realize the worthlessness of making complaints in the army.

Tjaden and Kropp are given light sentences in the open prison. But since the prisoners can be visited, it is not at all a hardship.

Kat and Baumer conspire to steal a goose. While Baumer tries to grab his prey, a bulldog attacks him. So he shoots the dog, snatches the goose, and makes off with it alongside Kat. They cook the bird without discussion, "but I believe we have a more complete communion with one another than even lovers have."

Baumer knows that before the war, he and Kat would have had nothing to do with each other. But the experience of war has brought them into an intimate pact—the sort of relationship that grants peace and comfort in an otherwise hostile atmosphere.

When the goose is cooked, they eat it together, then take some to Tjaden and Kropp.

Commentary

This chapter is important in its exposition of the comradeships that develop during the war. The men feel a close bond to one another and are prepared to stand up in defence for their friends when assaulted by idiots like Himmelstoss.

In their fantasies about peace-time, they all have different ideas about what they would do. Some are realistic (such as Detering, with his farm work), while others are more non-committal (Baumer sees life as being somewhat hopeless; Müller worries about their education; Westhus thinks of continuing in the army, etc.).

The full force of their comradeship is demonstrated when Tjaden stands up to Himmelstoss. The men, in unison, support their friend, and Kropp eventually spends time in prison for doing so. But it is worth it to them to put the autocratic postman in his place. It is part of the retribution process that we mentioned earlier in terms of karma.

Animals and animal imagery play a significant role in this novel. Here, we see Baumer in contest with two geese and a bulldog. The animals attempt to defend themselves against the aggressor Baumer, just as the Germans try to fend off the British. The struggle for survival is often illustrated in this animal/human being parallel. Since man is also an animal, the conflict takes on an even more poignant meaning. Animals are helpless against mankind. This is because man has the weapons and strength to defeat them.

But the same struggle takes place between men of opposing armies. Weaponry and strength are vital for victory, and the force with greater strength is likely to be the winner. The scenes of animal imagery serve to highlight this struggle in a symbolic, more visible fashion.

CHAPTER 6

Summary

With rumours of an offensive, the men go to the front two days earlier than usual. On their way, they pass a shelled school house, against which lean about a hundred new coffins. The men realize that these death-boxes are for them.

Life at the front is dangerous. It is like "a cage in which we must await fearfully whatever may happen. We lie under the network of arching shells and live in a suspense of uncertainty. Over us Chance hovers." It is this element of chance that makes them indifferent. Every soldier believes in luck and in his chances for being spared.

Baumer describes the condition of the trenches. They are in need of repair and have become infested with rats. The rodents eat their food and are repulsive. Finally the men can tolerate this no longer: they pile bits of bread in the center of the trench and wait for the rats to come. When this happens, each man strikes hard at them with his spade, and they repeat the process until the rats are under control.

The bayonet is no longer an important weapon. The men now use bombs and spades. The sharpened spade can split a man open as far down as his chest if he is hit between the neck and shoulder.

They are unable to figure out what the Allies are doing behind the line. Though the Germans fire on them continually, the Allied trains and trucks do not cease. Kat is gloomy about the situation. " 'It will be like the Somme.' " Day after day passes. Then, one night, they are awakened by flame-throwers. "The earth booms. Heavy fire is falling on us. We crouch into corners."

The bombardment continues and falls in the rear as well. "As far as one can see, it spouts fountains of mud and iron."

It is impossible for them to get food through to the line. The fighting is intense and the risk would be enormous. Towards morning, an onslaught of rats causes the soldiers to strike out viciously at the animals. This exhausts the already hungry, worn-out men. It mystifies the Germans where the Allies get all their shells.

Baumer and Kat prevent a young recruit from killing himself. The pressure is so great that the recruit goes crazy, anxious to hurl himself into the line of fire so as to end his pain. Finally they beat him in order to settle him down. Hopefully it will be a deterrent to other claustrophobic recruits.

Suddenly, their dugout is hit, though not seriously. Nonetheless, "the walls reel, rifles, helmets, earth, mud, and dust fly everywhere. Sulphur fumes pour in."

Night arrives and the bombardment has stopped. But Baumer realizes that the attack is about to begin: ". . . fifty yards from us a machine-gun is already in position and barking. The wire-entanglements are torn to pieces. Yet they offer some obstacle. We see the storm-troops coming. Our artillery opens fire." The fighting begins anew.

The attackers are French. Once inside the range of German artillery and machine-guns, the French suffer serious losses. Arms and legs dangle on barbed wire, while the rest of the bodies lie strewn across the field.

Baumer thinks of their actions as being necessary for survival. "We have become wild beasts. We do not fight, we defend ourselves against annihilation." He has nothing personal against any of the attackers since he does not know any of them. They represent only the entity that threatens to kill him. So, to prevent that, he must kill them. "If your own father came over with them you would not hesitate to fling a bomb at him."

They abandon the forward trenches, which have been bombed to bits. The Allied losses are considerable. They had not counted on such resistance from the Germans.

While in pursuit of some straggling Frenchmen, Baumer and his comrades reach the enemy line. "We are so close on the heels of our retreating enemies that we reach it almost at the same time as they." Kat smashes the face of an unwounded machine-gunner. They bayonet the others before they are able to throw bombs.

The fight ends and they lose touch with the Allied troops. The Germans seize everything they can from the abondoned trenches. Then they retreat quickly back to their own position.

That night, everyone is exhausted from the attack. Baumer's thoughts are more like memories than anything else; they focus on his home and make him nostalgic. He recalls the poplar trees along the stream and wonders whether, by the age of twenty, he will have known "the bewildering emotions of love."

His memories have a calming effect on Baumer. But he cannot allow himself to become too calm, lest he forget where he is. The threat of the front is real, and he must be prepared for action. It is easier to sink into fantasies of desire while in the barracks. Here in the trenches, all desire is gone. In its place lies a readiness for war.

Baumer speaks of the vast changes that have occured in the minds of the soldiers. They long for their former lives, but could they survive in them? Could they return to their families and function in the same way? "We are no longer untroubled—we are indifferent . . . . We are forlorn like children, and experienced like old men, we are crude and sorrowful and superficial—I believe we are lost."

This has been an exceptionally unnerving stay at the front. As the days go by, attacks alternate with counter-attacks, while the dead pile up. The soldiers collect the silken parachutes of the French star shells and send them home to their girl-friends. They can be made into blouses.

The shelling begins again. Most of the men to die are new recruits who have no sense of cover, no ear for sound and character of the shells. Between five and ten recruits die for every experienced soldier.

In one part of the trench, Baumer runs into Himmelstoss. They dive into the same dug-out and lie beside one another, breathless. When Baumer leaves the dug-out, he wonders where Himmelstoss is. So he returns and finds him in the dug-out, huddled in the corner, pretending to be wounded but actually in a panic. The front is new to him, too, but Baumer resents this lack of courage—particularly since new recruits are out there risking their lives.

Baumer tells Himmelstoss to come out, but the latter refuses. He is terrified. Baumer shakes him, kicks him and calls him various names, but the man still holds firm. Finally Baumer pushes him out head first. Once outside, Himmelstoss hears a lieutenant shout the command of " 'Forward, forward, join in, follow.' " This throws him back into his officer mentality.

Baumer has lost track of time. It has only been days since they've been at the front, but it seems like years. The experienced men teach the new recruits how to look after themselves. "They listen, they are docile—but when it begins again, in their excitement they do everything wrong."

Haie Westhus is badly wounded in the back. He calls to Baumer that the end is near and bites his arm because of the pain. It is a scene of bloody carnage—vile, hideous and inhuman.

The fighting has cost the Germans dearly. On every yard of lost land, there lies a dead soldier. But the Allies have only gained a few hundred yards.

Baumer's troop is relieved at the line. It was summer when they came up, and now it is autumn. The night is grey and wet. When the truck carrying Baumer arrives at its destination, Baumer gets out and recognizes Kat and Kropp. The three lean against each other, stunned by the atrocities. Only a very small number of men remain alive from their company. Thirty-two men have survived from the group of 150.

Commentary

This is the longest chapter so far, but perhaps the most simple to understand. Simple because it elaborates one major idea: war is a preposterous, savage death-trap in which all human dignity is destroyed.

By now, the principal characters have become real people for us. We have followed them through a series of interactions, and we care deeply about them. Each has his individuality and unique features, and we scrutinize his well-being as if we, too, were members of the company.

For this reason, we feel the wretchedness of their situation. This intensifies our reactions to the novel. The description of the rats and their intrusion in the trenches causes empathy and horror on our part. That human beings are subjected to these atrocities is something that we find difficult to imagine, especially if we have never been involved in a war.

Remarque uses the incident of the rats to show the balance of nature at work. In the Darwinian theory of the survival of the fittest, only the strong can survive when competition determines evolution. On one level, we have the Germans versus the Allies. It is a struggle that, at this point in the novel, has yet to be resolved. But on another level, there is conflict between the soldiers and the rats, between mankind and the animal world. Man proves to be smarter and stronger than the rats; hence, the rats are destroyed.

But on a third level, the rats that have survived are still hungry. They discover two large cats and a dog, mangle them to death, and devour them as food. Thus, rats become the winners in an evolutionary process confined to the animal world. We see how progressive levels of strength determine the degree of survival. But the weeding out by murder is no less savage on the human level than on the animal. This illustrates Remarque's viewpoint that civilization plays no part in war, that social niceties become irrelevant when the animal in man takes over.

On a more personal level, however, Baumer demonstrates his steady concern for individual human beings. He takes a young recruit into protection and prevents the youngster from being killed. Indeed, Baumer's sensitivities are so keen that he hesitates killing an enemy, a Frenchman, whom he sees at close range:

> Under one of the helmets a dark pointed beard and two eyes that are fastened on me. I raise my hand, but I cannot throw [a hand-grenade] into those strange eyes; for one mad moment the whole slaughter whirls like a circus round me, and these two eyes alone are motionless; then the head rises up, a hand, a movement, and my hand-grenade flies through the air and into him.

It is not because Baumer wishes to kill the Frenchman that he throws the grenade. As we have seen earlier, it is for reasons of survival that he must defend himself. He takes pity on the man for a while, seeing him as a fellow human being rather than as an Allied soldier. His mind shifts to a perceptive state where nationality counts for nothing—the atrocity and vulgarity of murder throw him into a confusion. But when the Frenchman makes a threatening move (*any* move would be threatening), Baumer has no choice. He must kill. That is the rule of the game.

As for Himmelstoss' cowardice, this is a predictable emotion in a man for whom we have had nothing but contempt. We have seen through his pettiness and discovered a heartless, corruptible soul determined to exploit his power at other people's expense. Now, the sudden fright on his part comes as the ultimate disgrace. He knows he has been caught. From this point on, he must live with this knowledge.

CHAPTER 7

Summary

The men are taken back farther than usual to a field depot so they can get reorganized. A couple of days later, Himmelstoss comes up to them. He has been jarred to reality by the action at the front and wants to be friends with them. Baumer is willing to go along with it since he witnessed Himmelstoss' concern for Westhus when the latter was shot in the back. The only one reluctant to change the relationship is Tjaden.

But even Tjaden gives way when Himmelstoss takes over as sergeant-cook while the latter goes on leave. Himmelstoss produces two pounds of sugar for them and a half-pound of butter for Tjaden. This convinces Tjaden of the man's good motives.

Baumer offers two insightful comments about human nature: (1) man is a creature of habit, and when he gets used to something, he can function quite well under those circumstances; (2) "terror can be endured so long as a man simply ducks;—but it kills, if a man thinks about it."

The men are billeted near the canal in houses that have been abandoned. They are not permitted to cross the canal to the other side, where occasionally they see inhabitants. One day, a group of soldiers is swimming nude in the canal when some French women stroll by. The men attempt to detain them in order to have some fun, but the women cannot pass onto the soldiers' territory. The women start walking away, but the soldiers swim after them. Finally, the women point to a house in the trees that belongs to them. The soldiers decide to visit them there at night when the guards on the bridges cannot see clearly.

The men will swim over to the women's house this evening. Since there are four soldiers and only three women, they decide to get Tjaden drunk. That way, he will not be able to accompany them.

Later that evening, the three men (Baumer, Kropp and Leer) swim across the canal, naked, with their boots packed with provisions for the women. When they arrive, the women take one look at them and laugh. Moments later, they give the soldiers some clothes and sympathize with them about the war: "La guerre—grand malheur—pauvres garçons—" ["War, what a tragedy, poor boys . . ."].

Baumer feels vulnerable with the brunette. He desires her but is lost in remoteness without his soldier's trappings. "Her mouth speaks words I do not understand. Nor do I fully understand her eyes; they seem to say more than we anticipated when we came here."

Baumer and the brunette make love. He lets all the horror and fears of war fall from him as he experiences his youth and a growing happiness. But when they leave, Baumer feels unfulfilled. "I cannot trust myself to speak, I am not in the least happy."

Before they are able to jump back into the canal, the three soldiers see another naked man, in boots, making his way to the women's house. It is Tjaden, and they laugh. They predict he will curse them in the morning.

Baumer is called to the Orderly Room, where he is issued a pass for fourteen days' leave. After that, he will report to a camp on the moors for a course of training. The others congratulate him, and Kat advises him to get a base job. Baumer feels nostalgic about his friends: will they still be alive when he returns? Already Haie Westhus has gone.

Baumer gets on the train and spends many an hour passing through villages that are familiar to him. Finally he arrives in his home town and makes his way home. His eldest sister, Erna, sees him and, in her excitement, shouts out to their mother.

I lean against the wall and grip my helmet and rifle. I

hold them as tight as I can, but I cannot take another step, the staircase fades before my eyes . . . my sister's call has made me powerless, I can do nothing, I struggle to make myself laugh, to speak, but no word comes, and so I stand on the steps, miserable, helpless, paralysed, and against my will the tears run down my cheeks.

His mother is ill but happy to see him. "She looks at me. Her hands are white and sickly and frail compared with mine. We say very little and I am thankful that she asks nothing."

But despite his familiar surroundings, Baumer can find nothing of himself at home. He feels strange, alienated, preoccupied. His mother asks him if it is very bad at the front, but Baumer prefers not to discuss it with her. He falsifies his answer and says: " 'No, Mother, not so very. There are always a lot of us together so it isn't so bad.' "

They have never been very open about their feelings in Baumer's family. As poor folk, they have toiled and struggled but nonetheless care deeply about one another. It's just that they express themselves verbally in a minimal way. Erna tells Baumer that their mother probably has cancer.

Baumer leaves the house and proceeds to the District Commandant to report. On his way back, an irate major demands that he be saluted by Baumer. He is an annoying authority figure, but Baumer knows that his leave depends on being polite with the man. The major tells him to leave his front-line manners at the line. Once Baumer has obeyed all the major's orders, the major dismisses him. But it has ruined the evening for Baumer.

He goes home and changes clothes, throwing the army uniform into the corner. His father wants him to remain in uniform so he can show Baumer off to his friends. But he refuses.

Baumer's rapport with his father has deteriorated. He no longer knows what to say to him. The man wants to discuss Baumer's traumas at the front line. Baumer notes that ". . . he is curious in a way that I find stupid and distressing; I no longer have any real contact with him."

Sitting in a beer garden, Baumer ponders the difference in life-styles between the civilian and front-line existences. His

German-master approaches him and drags him off to another table where a group of people discuss the war. It is conversation that does not interest him. They represent value systems that differ considerably from his own. These are the people who keep nations at war. They talk of aggressive behaviour and acquisition of foreign territories, etc. They are the authority figures whom Baumer has grown to despise.

The German-master indicates his ideas about how the breakthrough in France can take place. Baumer replies that such a breakthrough may not be possible. A stalemate has existed along the Western Front since the war's beginning, and no signs of change are in sight.

The master informs Baumer arrogantly that he knows nothing about the war. Baumer chooses to break away from the conversation. The master stuffs a few cigars in Baumer's pocket and tells him: " 'All of the best! I hope we will soon hear something worth while from you.' "

Baumer knows that his leave differs greatly from the leave he had one year ago. Or rather, *he* differs from the man he was then. "At that time I still knew nothing about the war, we had only been in quiet sectors. But now I see that I have been crushed without knowing it. I find I do not belong here any more, it is a foreign world."

Baumer resents the attitude of the people around him. They all think they understand what the war is about, but their understanding is a product of their imagination. He prefers to remain alone so that no one can trouble him. Their desires and problems no longer interest him, even though a year ago, these were his worries too. People tend to see things in extremes: the war is either this way or that way, and everyone has the perfect explanation. This troubles Baumer.

In the privacy of his bedroom, Baumer looks at his schoolbooks and becomes excited about that period of his life, even though he feels that ". . . I do not want to be, for that is not right. I want that quiet rapture again." The allure of learning excites him, and he looks forward to recapturing the powerful urge of eagerness. He wants an end to the war, a "great homecoming tide."

But as he stares at the books, he feels nothing. No intensity, no curiosity—nothing. The spark is gone. "A terrible feeling of foreignness suddenly rises up in me." He is shut out from his past. He opens the books in search of hope but finds only words; the words do not reach him.

Baumer goes to see a friend in the barracks. Mittelstaedt tells him that Kantorek has been called up as a territorial [a member of the force designed to serve in home defence to replace older bodies of militia; a territorial has very little authority]. Kantorek had approached Mittelstaedt with a chummy attitude and the latter replied to him: " 'Territorial Kantorek, business is business and schnapps is schnapps, you ought to know that well enough. Stand to attention when you speak to a superior officer.' " Kantorek, the proverbial idealist about war, was horrified. But Mittelstaedt did not relent; instead, he snubbed him harder.

Mittelstaedt reminded Kantorek that two years earlier he had persuaded the young men to enlist. The one boy, Josef Behm, who had not wanted to enlist was killed three months before he would have been called up in the ordinary manner. Had it not been for Kantorek, Behm would have lived longer. With that, Mittelstaedt dismissed Kantorek and informed him that: " 'You will hear from me later.' "

Mittelstaedt leads Baumer out to the parade-ground where he intends to inspect his company. Baumer stifles his laughter as he sees Kantorek in a faded blue tunic, badly tailored to his body. Soon, Mittelstaedt approaches Kantorek and blasts him for his unpolished buttons. Baumer bubbles with glee. " 'Inadequate, Kantorek, quite inadequate—' " These were the very words that Kantorek had used on Mittelstaedt in school. Baumer grins at Kantorek "as though I do not recognize him any more." The scene is quite comical, though also pathetic.

Mittelstaedt parrots phrases to Kantorek that the schoolmaster had once thundered at his classes. " 'Territorial Kantorek, we have the good fortune to live in a great age, we must brace ourselves and triumph over hardship.' "

As his leave draws to a close, Baumer goes to visit Kemmerich's mother. The woman is bitter about her son's death and reproaches Baumer for still being alive. She wants to know how Franz was killed. Baumer states that he was shot through the heart and died instantly, yet she doubts him. We recall that Kemmerich died a slow, agonizing death after his leg amputation. Somehow his mother knows that Baumer is lying about the shot through the heart. She tells him: " 'You lie. I know better.' '' The woman is certain of herself: Baumer has falsified the story. Call it ESP or woman's intuition— the point is, she senses something amiss.

The night before Baumer's leave ends, he goes to bed and pretends to be asleep when his mother enters the room. She sits there for a long time. Then he tells her to get some sleep. She asks if he is afraid, and he replies no. He thinks to himself that her love and comfort are so necessary to him, but he must not confide this in her. He would love to rise up with her and go back in time to the period when they were alone, unthreatened by war. It is a scene of point counterpoint in that he tells her what she wants to hear, but he thinks something quite different.

Baumer ushers her back to her room. "How destitute she lies there in her bed, she that loves me more than all the world." He is tremendously sad at the prospect of having to be separated from her. Before he leaves the room, she gives him two pairs of woolen underpants. Baumer knows that they must have cost his mother a great deal in terms of waiting, walking and begging.

Baumer regrets having come home on leave. At the front, he was indifferent about life; things seemed hopeless. Now he has experienced emotion again and sees himself as an agony "for myself, for my mother, for everything that is so comfortless and without end."

Commentary

This is the longest chapter in the novel and, in many ways, the most complicated. It stands quite nicely as a unity, but it is in fact an ensemble of several movements of thought. There are six principal points that we need to look at in order to understand this chapter.

1. The law of cause and effect: We have seen how Himmelstoss treated his soldiers in a nasty, degrading fashion and, as a result of this behaviour, lost their respect. We mentioned the law of cause and effect, represented by the notion of karma, as an inescapable universal rule that governs human life. What we give is what we get.

In the case of Himmelstoss, he treated his men badly and, in turn, they treat him in the same way. By being negative, he attracts negativity to himself. Likewise, Kantorek is thrown into this system of karma in Chapter 7. As a schoolmaster, he has treated his students with great authority and supremacy. He has forced them to believe certain values and ideas that otherwise may not have been theirs. Because of his preaching, they enlist in the army without even thinking about the consequences. The men realize later that they erred by placing such unqualified trust in Kantorek's philosophies. They resent him for his brainwashing and vow to reject his kind of influence.

So, in keeping with the law of cause and effect, Kantorek cannot escape the punishment headed his way. It comes via a former student of his, Mittelstaedt, who now has authority over him in the army and who causes him to recall, word for word, his lofty, unrealistic classroom commands.

Kantorek, like Himmelstoss, is punished as severely as his influence was negative on the young soldiers. In other words, the negative consequences come back at him as strenuously as they were emitted from him. If we could measure this cause/effect phenomenon quantitatively, it might go something like this: for every five units of negativity expended by someone, five units of negativity would return to this person.

This law works, not primarily as a form of punishment, but as a means by which people can learn from their mistakes. This is the principle demonstrated by Remarque. The author shows us Himmelstoss as a tyrant and as the recipient of tyrannical behaviour from his soldiers. Then he shows us Kantorek as a schoolroom tyrant and as the recipient of this attitude from Mittelstaedt.

When Mittelstaedt takes pleasure in disciplining Kantorek, Baumer says:

It amazes me that Kantorek does not explode with a bang, especially when, during physical exercises, Mittelstaedt copies him to perfection, seizing him by the seat of his trousers as he is pulling himself up on the horizontal bar so that he can just raise his chin above the beam, and then starts to give him good advice. *That is exactly what Kantorek used to do to him at school.* [my italics]

This last sentence is a direct illustration of Remarque's belief in the concept of cause and effect. And he goes even further. He shows that Himmelstoss, having been humiliated by his men, learns his lesson from the experience. He has benefited from the trauma and, as a result, the humiliation is no longer necessary. He attempts to become friendly with the soldiers and they accept his gesture. He gains dignity in the process and becomes a changed man.

The same fate awaits Kantorek if he chooses to alter his behaviour. But if he refuses and maintains a posture of arrogant authority, the principle of karma will continue its work on him. The negative boomerang effect will assault him until he becomes more genuine, more positive, more human.

It is not the term "karma" or its origins that count here. Rather, it is the idea behind it that interests Remarque and that helps the reader to understand this novel. Men who have fought in war claim that luck plays a great role in their survival. "Luck" can be interchanged with "fate," "cause and effect," or other terms. The point is, a positive action attracts a positive result, and the same is true with negativity. Remarque is careful to show us this principle at work with both Himmelstoss and Kantorek.

2. Sex and sociability: The soldiers, having left civilization, spend almost all of their time alone or with other men. This creates an emotional imbalance since all input from women in their lives is absent. The love, tenderness, caring and concern from their mothers, sisters, girl-friends, etc., is wrenched from their emotional orbit. This deprives them of fulfillment and a sense of completeness. Physically, mentally, emotionally and sexually, their life-style has changed.

When the men see the French women along the canal, this provides an outlet for them. Many of them have not wanted to patronize the brothels and, in the case of Baumer, the French women offer the chance of intimacy—both physical and emotional.

When the sex drive is repressed, as in times of war, or altered from its customary expression, the results are predictable: tension, frustration, loneliness and a profound sense of separation from "normal" life. This is what makes the episode with the French women important: they represent a transition to civilized life for Baumer and a reminder that he has deep feelings that have gone unattended.

Baumer is a likeable, honest man of integrity. We come to like him as his story unravels and we trust his judgment. We see the characters and events through his eyes. For this reason, we experience with him the difficult and sensitive transition to civilian life. It is his sexual encounter with the French woman that moves him away from the army and back to sociability.

But during his leave, he comes full cycle and regrets having left the front line. He was indifferent to its hardships, from force of habit, and now feels the rage of emotions inside. This renewed contact with human warmth and love takes on an ironical meaning when, at the chapter's end, his mother cautions him about French women: " '. . . be on your guard against the women out in France. They are no good.' "

The French women had symbolized a return to civilization. Now, as he re-enters the army life, he is warned about this symbol of civilization. We recall Baumer's feeling of unhappiness the night he departed from the French woman's arms. And now, as he moves back in that direction, he is equally unhappy.

The message here is: war has a strong impact on the sexual and social life of a soldier. His ability to interact in "normal" peace-time settings is inhibited, and he feels trapped by inadequacy. This leads us to the third principal point of this chapter.

3. Alienation of the soldier in civilian life: In general, the soldier experiences a sensation of alienation and shock as he attempts to re-enter his former life-style. Baumer suffers from shellshock when he hears the screeching of the tram cars. He is without friends since most of them are either dead or still at the front. He is subjected to insults from both army and civilian individuals and feels worthless as a human being.

The German-master in the beer garden has all the answers to the war. He represents the kind of person whom the soldiers distrust: those who are removed from the action and speak arrogantly of its meaning; who ask questions about subjects that Baumer wishes to forget and fail to respect his need for privacy.

Even Baumer's father is in error on that account. He wants Baumer to remain in military uniform so that he can show him off to his friends. The father thinks of himself, not of his son, and is part of that generation that spoke romantically of the war.

The obnoxious major who stops Baumer and makes him salute properly is but another example of hated authority. Even on leave, Baumer is unable to escape the imposition of haughtiness associated with the military hierarchy. It becomes something of a nightmare, which haunts Baumer wherever he goes. The only way to overcome it is to get into civilian clothes, throw his uniform in a corner, and, symbolically, put the war behind him.

So here we have a man who is uncomfortable with his return home since he has become separated from army friends and since civilians fail to understand the pressures under which he has lived. To aggravate matters, his father puts pressure on him, an anonymous major dictates orders to him and people in a beer garden talk in theoretical terms about a very real war.

These factors serve to alienate Baumer from his former surroundings. This leaves him in a precarious situation: he wants the war to end, yet he is alienated from his former existence. No matter what direction he moves in, there is conflict and uncertainty. Hence, discouragement, frustration and, ultimately, a sense of worthlessness.

4. The irrelevance of nationality: It makes no difference to Baumer and his friends that the three women by the canal are French. The war is a monstrous game plotted out by high-ranking officials and members of government. Soldiers are merely the pawns of power. Reduced to this status, they lack even the most fundamental of human rights.

We have seen that the soldier's desire to kill an enemy stems less from enjoyment of murder than from a keen need to survive. The threat of annihilation causes him to strike out against his rival. But when the threat is absent (as it was when Baumer first noticed a Frenchman's eyes peering at him on the battlefield), there is no need to kill.

Similarly, the absence of threat with the French women allow Baumer and his friends to forget about the war. They are able to focus on human interaction. Nationality is irrelevant. Remarque stated many times over, after the publication of this novel, that he sought only to expose war for what it did to human beings. He was not for or against Germany or England or France or Russia. Rather, he aimed to bring out the vulgar atrocities of the process and horrify people with the psychology behind it.

Human beings, not individual nations, are what interested Remarque. It was of little importance that the women by the canal were French—other than to point out that language, culture and rules can do nothing to undermine the basic need for human expression.

5. Absence of the father: It is worth noting that Baumer's father, with rare exceptions, is almost totally absent from this chapter. We may conclude that the man is likewise absent from his son's life, other than at moments when Baumer can serve some egotistic purpose for him. Baumer's emotional reactions to the leave are defined primarily by his contact with his dying mother. They experience an understated warmth and love for one another, which bring the chapter to a moving conclusion. But the father is merely someone who passes through Baumer's life by necessity. If he has been important to Baumer, this is in no way clarified by the chapter.

The mother represents emotion, love and concern—that is, the safety of a home life away from the war. The father derives pleasure from his son's experience as a soldier; he becomes associated, as a result, with the war. So, in choosing between his mother (anti-war) and his father (pro-war), Baumer prefers his mother. We are not suggesting that the father is necessarily in favour of the war. But, insofar as his relationship with his son is concerned, he exhibits positive reactions to Baumer's association with the army.

6. Extra-sensory perception (ESP): It is clear that Remarque was intrigued by the powers of the mind. The mind, or psyche, is central to Remarque's explanation of the unconscious forces embedded within each of us—the idea that the unconscious mind functions more powerfully than the conscious mind and is of greater use to a soldier in times of emergency.

In Chapter 7, Remarque goes one step further and demonstrates the phenomenon of extra-sensory perception. When Baumer tells Kemmerich's mother about her son's death, he wishes to downplay the agony of Franz's final moments. He fabricates a tale about the gunshot wound through Kemmerich's heart and claims the boy died instantly. Mrs. Kemmerich doubts that this is true. She manifests an assertive, desperate need for truth and begs Baumer to give her the facts.

She tells him: " 'You lie. . . . I have felt how terribly he died. I have heard his voice at night, I have felt his anguish—tell the truth, I want to know it, I must know it.' " As with the term "karma," the precise label of Mrs. Kemmerich's emotion is not important here. Whether it be intuition, ESP, or some other form of psychic insight, the fact remains that she knows Baumer is lying. She has been the receptor of some type of communication about Franz. Only the truth will put her mind to rest.

Ironically, she demands as proof that Baumer is telling the truth his sacred oath, sworn to her, that Franz died instantly. She demands of him: " 'Are you willing never to come back yourself, if it isn't true?' " It is like a spell that she casts over him, which augurs badly if he dares to lie. His reply is: " 'May I never come back if he wasn't killed instantaneously.' " The irony—or is it irony?—lies in Baumer's ultimate fate. We shall see at the novel's end that there is a link between his oath to Mrs. Kemmerich and Baumer's final destiny.

CHAPTER 8

Summary
When Baumer returns to the camp on the moors, he discovers it has changed since his last visit there. He goes through the routine mechanically and has very few acquaintances. But this is quite acceptable to him; he is not anxious to form friendships.

Next to the camp is a Russian prison camp separated by a wire fence. But the Russian prisoners come into the German camp and pick over the garbage tins. Baumer notices them up close and finds them kind. This reinforces what we have already said about the irrelevance of nationality. He is troubled, however, by their impoverished state. They are weak, hungry and captives without power. Almost every day, one of the Russians dies. They are buried quickly and with little ado.

Since Baumer has had a long leave, he is not granted leave on Sundays. His father and sister come to visit, and they discuss his mother's illness. The hours are a torture for Baumer since no one knows what to talk about.

Commentary
This is a short chapter with one major idea: Baumer feels empathy for the Russian prisoners and expresses concern for their welfare. He treats them as human beings, not as enemies, and wishes they could communicate better.

Baumer has gone to this training camp because he needs a refresher course before returning to the front. It is customary to prepare the soldiers for action if they have been inactive for several days.

Baumer sees beyond nationality and appreciates the condition of the Russian prisoners. He perceives in them a fundamental state of misery that is common to all human beings: ". . . I perceive behind them only the suffering of the creature, the awful melancholy of life and the pitilessness of men."

This chapter is necessary as a transition from civilian life back to the horrors of war. It is less intense than Chapter 7, but we sense a growing anxiety that will evolve in the next section of the novel.

CHAPTER 9

Summary

Baumer travels for a few days, then arrives back at the company barracks. He sees Tjaden, Müller, Kat and Kropp. It is good to be back with them and this is where he belongs, but a strange guilt creeps over him. He has been on leave while they have fought battles. Rumour has it that they are going to Russia. But Baumer thinks: "To Russia? It's not much of a war over there." The Eastern Front is not as threatening as the Western Front.

The men are outfitted in new uniforms because the Kaiser is coming to inspect them. The Kaiser is disappointing in size and power: he is not the great man they had imagined him to be.

The men discuss the subject of which nation is right in the struggle for victory: France or Germany? Each country claims to be in the right, so how can one know for sure? Baumer comments: " 'That I don't know, . . . but whichever way it is there's war all the same and every month more countries coming in.' " Tjaden wonders how war is caused, and Kropp answers: " 'Mostly by one country badly offending another.' "

Tjaden cannot agree with Kropp. He does not believe himself to be offended at all by the French and cannot see why he should be at war. He feels no affinity to the State, though he loves his home country. There is a big difference. The politicians who make the decisions and who thrust the country into war are not the ones, necessarily, who represent the will of the people.

Kat states: " '. . . just you consider, almost all of us are simple folk. And in France, too, the majority of men are labourers, workmen, or poor clerks. Now just why would a French blacksmith or a French shoemaker want to attack us? No, it is merely the rulers.' " Tjaden cannot understand who needs war, including the Kaiser who has everything he could ever want. But Kat disagrees: " '. . . he has not had a war up till now. And every full-grown emperor requires at least one war, otherwise he would not become famous.' "

Instead of going to Russia, they go back to the front line. On their way, they pass through a devastated section of land where dead soldiers hang from trees. Limbs are scattered everywhere. The massacre has taken place recently, so the men waste no time in reporting the carnage.

Baumer volunteers to go on the patrol that will determine how far the enemy position is advanced. It is the first patrol since his leave, and he is quite frightened. But soon he hears the familiar voices of his comrades and this reassures him.

I am no longer a shuddering speck of existence, alone in the darkness;—I belong to them and they to me; we all share the same fear and the same life, we are nearer than lovers, in a simpler, a harder way; I could bury my face in them, in these voices, these words that have saved me and will stand by me.

Shortly afterward, Baumer loses his sense of direction and no longer knows where to go. He may be moving parallel to the line—a process that could continue forever. He realizes that ". . . to crawl in the right direction is a matter of life or death." A bombardment begins and machine-guns rattle. He decides to lie low. But the new threat is the advancing Allied army, which could come upon him and murder him. Baumer lowers himself into mud water up to his head, pretends to be dead, and prepares himself with a knife in case an Allied soldier should jump into the water near him.

The Germans repel the Allies and Baumer is saved. But then a soldier falls over him into the shell-hole and lies across him. Baumer stabs him to death in a effort to prevent any noise from being heard. He cannot escape because it is too light out. The machine-gun fire sweeps the ground very low, and he would be shot to death. He supposes that his comrades have given him up for lost.

Baumer hears a gurgle coming from the "dead" man. He realizes that the soldier is not dead and is attempting to move. The man has terror in his eyes: "The body lies still, but in the eyes there is such an extraordinary expression of fright that for a moment I think they have power enough to carry the body off with them." Baumer feels dreadful about the poor man and tries to comfort him, all the while telling him to remain quiet.

Baumer knows the man will die but dresses his wounds anyway. "This is the first time I have killed with my hands, whom I can see close at hand, whose death is my doing." The man dies at about three in the afternoon.

The agony of having killed a man deprives Baumer of peace of mind. He thinks of the soldier's wife, of the letters that the man probably sent to her. He wishes that Kantorek were sitting next to him. In despair, he begins speaking to the dead man and offers his regrets.

Baumer takes the man's wallet from his shirt in order to identify him. He intends to write to his wife, parents and child. He wishes to take care of them. But he also knows that once he identifies the dead man by name, the man will become imprinted on his memory. He will never be able to forget him. The Frenchman's wallet falls to the ground, and letters and photographs scatter everywhere. When Baumer translates parts of the letters, he is heart-broken by what he has done.

He vows to himself that he will send money to the man's family. The man's name was Gérard Duval, and he was a printer. "I have killed the printer, Gérard Duval. I must be a printer, I think confusedly, be a printer, printer—"

Time passes and Baumer settles down; his madness changes to resolution. He is bitter about the fighting that propelled him and the Frenchman into this senseless battle. He promises to protest against war if he comes out of it alive. His life will never be the same.

Baumer has not eaten for more than a day, yet he cannot escape the shell-hole. But when night falls, he scurries from shell-hole to shell-hole, calling out his name and waiting for an answer from his comrades. Kat and Kropp call back to him; they have come looking for him with a stretcher.

The next morning, he tells Kat and Kropp about the dead printer. They calm him with understanding words.

Commentary

This chapter is devoted primarily to a discussion of war: its philosophy and implications to human beings.

When Baumer returns to the front, he enters a conversation with his friends about the nature of war. They offer various viewpoints, but Tjaden's is the one that everyone agrees with. Tjaden places the blame for war on the powerful authority figures, represented by the State, and claims that these figures are quite different from those who love the homeland. Tjaden wants nothing to do with these statesmen. They are hungry for power and willing to waste millions of lives in order to attain it.

The discussion takes on a symbolic importance when the Kaiser comes to inspect them. Here is a man whom most of them have held in awe and respect, mostly because one thinks of one's leaders as being omnipotent and wise. But Baumer describes their reactions to the Kaiser: "He stalks along the line, and I am really rather disappointed; judging from his pictures I imagined him to be bigger and more powerfully built, and above all to have a thundering voice."

The reality of the Kaiser does not fit the illusion. The same is true of war. While many enjoy war as a theoretical, romantic game of power and strategy, those who actually fight in it see things differently. It is a seamy, wretched assault on human dignity. And, as with most aspects of life, the poor and humble must do the dirty work for the rich and powerful. This is the message of the men's conversation about war.

The occasion of Gérard Duval's murder draws us back again to the sensitivity of Paul Baumer. He despairs at having deprived another human being of his life and, with blood-stained hands, realizes the atrocity of his actions. Yet he had no choice, within the context of war, and was faced with the difficult situation of killing or being killed.

The passage with Gérard Duval brings out more clearly than any other in the novel the idea of victimization: the soldiers are victims of their State, of their country's political régimes, and must serve the homeland according to instructions. Freedom of choice is gone and so is the notion of individual responsibility. One ceases to function as a human being in order that a group mentality can collectively victimize the enemy. Regardless of one's perspective, victimization is the inevitable outcome of war.

CHAPTER 10

Summary

The men are positioned in an abandoned village, which has

70

been heavily shelled. They must guard the village and, in particular, the supply dump. They provide beds and blankets for themselves from the village, and find all sorts of food in the vacated houses. They begin eating at two and finish at six. It is a marvellous feast—one that they have had to duck shells for in order to enjoy.

They spend almost two weeks enjoying this life-style: eating, drinking and roaming about. They enjoy themselves more than at any other time during the war and hope to remain here until the fighting stops.

Eight days later, they are ordered to return to the front. They take with them a four-poster bed and two red armchairs, along with several bags of food.

After few days, they are sent to evacuate a village in which there are still some inhabitants. The French have made it a rule not to shell villages with inhabitants, but on this occasion, shell-fire strikes the rearguard of Baumer's column. He and Kropp dive for shelter in a ditch of mud. They wade in up to their necks and are soon exhausted. Kropp has been hit in the leg.

When they make a run for it, the shelling follows them. They reach a small dug-out. Baumer, too, has been wounded, and the two men help each other with bandages. An ambulance picks them up and takes them to a dressing-station. Kropp states emphatically that, if they amputate his leg, he will put an end to his life. He does not want to be a cripple for life.

A doctor operates on Baumer and removes a piece of shell. Baumer is told that he will be sent home the next day. The train arrives in the morning to take Baumer and Kropp home. The two are put in the same car and looked after by a Red Cross nurse.

Kropp has a fever and is to be put off the train at the next stop. So that they can remain together, Baumer fakes a fever by holding his breath and causing his face to redden. The two are sent to the Catholic Hospital and placed in the same room. They are annoyed the next morning when some nuns wake them up with their prayers. Baumer throws a bottle out the door; it smashes and causes the nuns to stop their noise.

When a hospital inspector arrives to determine who threw the bottle, a man quickly takes the blame for it. Later, Baumer asks him why he did this. The man replies that " 'I got a crack in the head and they presented me with a certificate to say that I was periodically not responsible for my actions. Ever since then I've had a grand time.' " The man's name is Josef Hamacher.

Another man in the ward, Franz Wächter, appears to be recovering from his wound. But one night, he notices a hemorrhage and asks Baumer to summon the night nurse. They get no response. Finally she arrives and scolds them for not having called her sooner. A discussion ensues during which Baumer finds out about the Dying Room. This is a place where men are taken so they can die. It can be a terrifying experience. One has no choice about the matter, and when it is clear that the man is being taken to that room, he realizes that the medical team has given up hope on him.

Baumer is operated on and vomits for two days. Kropp is seriously ill. They have amputated his leg at the thigh and he vows to shoot himself at the first possible moment.

Baumer realizes that the only way to understand the true agony of war is to see the hospitals. Every possible type of wound is visible, and Remarque spares no details in his descriptions of them.

Kropp's stump heals well, and he overcomes his anxiety about the amputation. Baumer's wounds heal also, and he is sent home on convalescent leave. His mother does not want to let him go. She is feeble, and things are much worse at home than during the last leave.

He is ordered back to the base after his convalescence and returns once more to the line. It was not easy to say goodbye to his friend Kropp, "But a man gets used to that sort of thing in the army."

Commentary

This is a chapter of sharp contrasts and one that prepares us for the conclusion of the novel.

In the first section, Baumer and his comrades enjoy a light, almost frivolous stay in an abandoned village. Despite the threat of nearby war, they take pleasure in their luxurious surroundings (i.e., rudimentary furniture) and ample stock of food. They engage in humorous role-playing, during which they treat each other as servants, valets, etc. It is a relief from the constant pressures of the line and, symbolically, shows two worlds in contradiction with one another: the stable, civilized home life symbolized by domestic furnishings and staples alongside the torturing struggle of life on the front.

But their light-hearted moments come to an end, and they are sent back to battle. This leads us to the second division of this chapter: the injuries, hospital rooms, convalescence and return to action. We have seen before in the novel evidence of grotesque carnage which shocks human sensitivity. The maimed, ruined human bodies that rip apart during warfare fill many a page in this wrenching drama. But the hospital scenes bring us one step closer to the ultimate indignities that await the wounded soldiers. It is not bad enough that they have endured suffering and pain on the battlefield; once they arrive at the hospital, they must often fight again for their lives against the self-righteous, tyrannical medical staff.

Operations are performed that need not be done. Patients are carted off like refuse to the Dying Room, despite their pleas to remain with friends. Nurses and doctors use the wounded as guinea pigs for personal experimentation. The list goes on and on. It is a haunting, traumatic world of nightmares, which frequently hastens, rather than preventing, the dying process.

A most significant passage in this chapter occurs at the end, where Baumer confesses his gut reactions to war:

I am young, I am twenty years old; yet I know nothing of life but despair, death, fear, and fatuous superficiality cast over an abyss of sorrow. I see how peoples are set against one another, and in silence, unknowingly, foolishly, obediently, innocently slay one another. I see that the keenest brains of the world invent weapons and words to make it yet more refined and enduring. And all men of my age, here and over there, throughout the whole world see these things; all my generation is experiencing these things with me. What would our fathers do if we suddenly stood up and came before them and proffered our account? What do they expect of us if a time ever comes when the war is over? Through the years our business has been killing;—it was our first calling in life. Our knowledge of life is limited to death. What will happen afterwards? And what shall come out of us?

This, more than any other passage in the novel, sums up the philosophy and attitude of Remarque toward war. It is a senseless, selfish, victimizing scandal, which plummets millions of people into murderous chaos. There can be no defence of a process in which the ambitious declare war only in order to glorify themselves and their governments. And, in the eyes of Remarque, there can be no solution to war other than to avoid its destruction by abstaining from its horrors.

CHAPTER 11

Summary

When Baumer first got to the front, it was winter. Now it is spring, and his life alters between direct action on the front and reserve duty in the billets. Though the men are transformed by nature into animal-like creatures, they benefit from a sense of brotherhood and mutual support. Their lives are constantly in jeopardy, and they must react objectively to the stresses around them: ". . . life is simply one continual watch against the menace of death;—it has transformed us into unthinking animals in order to give us the weapon of instinct—it has reinforced us with dullness, so that we do not go to pieces before the horror. . . ."

Baumer tells the story of Detering, who sees a cherry tree in full blossom and brings some branches back to the barracks. His behaviour is peculiar so Baumer keeps an eye on him. Two days later, Detering has vanished and is missed at roll call. Baumer knows that the cherry tree made Detering homesick for his farm and that he probably tried to escape in the direction of Germany. Nothing more has been heard of Detering.

The front line has been broken by the English. The Germans are surrounded and find it difficult to surrender. Müller is dead. He was shot point blank in the stomach. Even the company commander, Bertinck, falls. "He was one of those superb front-line officers who are foremost in every hot place. He was with us for two years without being wounded, so that something had to happen in the end."

Then Leer is hit and bleeds profusely from the hip. "Like an emptying tube, after a couple of minutes he collapses." Baumer wonders what use it is now to Leer that he was so good in math at school.

The summer of 1918 is the most bloody and atrocious ever. Human life is being annihilated everywhere. The German soldiers know that they are losing the war. But they keep fighting nonetheless, despite the huge losses and inevitable defeat. What the men want now, more than anything else, is life. They are tired of death, tired of struggling with waste. "Summer of 1918—Never was so much silently suffered as in the moment when we depart once again for the front-line."

Rumours of peace and armistice haunt the air and make it even harder for the men to return to the front. They want to live, but wonder if their lives will be absurdly robbed from them just as peace settles on the horizon.

The situation looks bad for the Germans; they have little food or ammunitions and their weapons are inadequate. "The rifles are caked, the uniforms caked, everything is fluid and dissolved, the earth one dripping, soaked, oily mass in which lie yellow pools with red spiral streams of blood and into which the dead, wounded, and survivors slowly sink down." It is a sordid, grinding mess.

One late summer day, Kat is wounded in the shin. Baumer lifts his friend onto his back and carries him to a dressing-station. The going is very difficult and dangerous. They rest in a shell-hole, and Baumer becomes very sad about the prospects of being separated, perhaps permanently, from his best friend. They exchange addresses, then set out again for the dressing-station. When they arrive, Baumer is trembling from the strain.

Baumer is relieved to have saved his friend. But the orderly takes one look at Kat and says: " 'You might have spared yourself that.' " Baumer questions him, only to discover that Kat has died in transit. Without Baumer's knowledge of it, Kat was hit by a small splinter in the head and has bled to death.

Slowly, Baumer comes to realize what has happened. He is stunned by Kat's death and accepts Kat's few belongings from the lance-corporal. In a moment of confusion, Baumer loses track of reality and sinks into a deep metaphysical trance. "Do I walk? Have I feet still? I raise my eyes, I let them move round, and turn myself with them, one circle, one circle, and I stand in the midst. All is as usual. Only the Militiaman Stanislaus Katczinsky has died."

Commentary

This chapter is the last stage of the vast psychological drama that has unfolded before us. In it, we see the final moments of the German attempt at victory, the demoralized, weakened forces trying valiantly to fulfill an impossible goal. There is no question that the Germans have lost, and now we witness the proud, dignified human efforts to validate this treacherous, bloody process. One overlooks one's nationality or political beliefs in favour of the psychological truth behind each word in Remarque's novel.

The brotherhood and mutual support among the soldiers is a phenomenon worthy of the highest human achievement. Men who otherwise might never have spoken to each other have become, by virtue of horror and despair, vital entities to the survival of their brothers. It is this unfailing sense of devotion, this selfless giving of love, that makes the dénouement all the more painful to accept.

Germany is, at this point, in the throes of defeat. Her armies are depleted, her supplies and ammunition insufficient and her soldier morale at an all-time low. "Every man here knows that we are losing the war. Not much is said about it, we are falling back, we will not be able to attack again after this big offensive, we have no more men and no more ammunition."

But to the credit of this broken army, the soldiers maintain pride in themselves—even on a remote, unconscious level—and demonstrate by their actions that they are part of a cause. The cause may be despicable and entirely without meaning. But they give it a meaning—*their* meaning—by collaborating with other human participants. "We are not beaten, for as soldiers we are better and more experienced; we are simply crushed and driven back by overwhelming superior forces."

The dénouement happens quickly. Major characters are struck down, the country loses ground, the back-up support dwindles and the soldiers are left with an unending hopelessness. "We have given up hope that some day an end may come." Historically, we can see that they are very close to the end of the fighting. It is 1918 and peace is on the way. But the soldiers do not know this yet. Peace is not peace until an agreement has been reached. So their loss of hope reflects a sentiment of the front line: as long as the fighting must continue, all hope remains lost.

When Bertinck falls, it is symbolic of the end. The company commander has not played an important role in the novel, but his presence as a leader is significant. Once the leader is shot down, the company is vulnerable to confusion and depression. The law of averages is at work insofar as the soldiers' thinking is concerned: they know that too much of a good thing cannot last. This is what prompts Baumer to say: "He was with us for two years without being wounded, so that something had to happen in the end."

The friendship between Baumer and Kat is a thing of great beauty in the history of literature. Their friendship is based on love and deep respect for one another, and highlights for us the countless similar relationships that developed during the war, during *any* war. When Baumer carries his beloved friend to the dressing-station, it is on one level an empty gift, since Kat is already dead. But on a more important level, he has transported his comrade to a more dignified final resting place than the muddy blood-bath of No Man's Land.

Each reader will react in a private, unique manner to this chapter. It sums up the driving intensity of Remarque's stance on war. Any event that ruins human lives, human relationships, human monuments and human accomplishments is an event that mankind must strive at all costs to avoid.

Yet war continues and so does death. Greed, and a lusting for power seem somehow more important to some than the preservation of human dignity.

CHAPTER 12

Summary

It is autumn. Baumer is the only one of the seven classmates who is still alive. Talk of peace is rampant, and everyone is counting on it. If the peace talks break up, there will be revolution.

Baumer is on a temporary leave since he swallowed some gas. He sits in the sunshine and thinks of armistice. He wants to go home.

He is hungry for life but has no aims. He is weary and rootless, without direction or hope. He anticipates a feeling of alienation and believes his generation of fighters will be ignored by society.

In the peace of the garden, Baumer watches the poplar trees and the berries of the rowan.

> I stand up. I am very quiet. Let the months and years come, they can take nothing from me, they can take nothing more. I am so alone, and so without hope that I can confront them without fear. The life that has borne me through these years is still in my hands and my eyes. . . . so long as it is there it will seek its own way out, heedless of the will that is within me.

In the last two paragraphs of this very short chapter, we discover that Baumer was killed in October 1918 on a day that was so quiet and still on the Western Front "that the army report confined itself to the single sentence: All quiet on the Western Front." He was found with a calm expression on his face and had apparently not suffered long. It looked as though he were "almost glad the end had come."

Commentary

This short chapter is more of an epitaph than anything else. It is intense, moving and pure poetry. The two principal ideas contained in it are: (1) peace can be so close, yet so far, and unless a state of peace has been formally declared, lives are still in jeopardy and will continue to be lost; (2) war victims and soldiers are often re-victimized by their countrymen when they return to civilian life after a war.

The lack of understanding on the part of civilians toward returning soldiers is perhaps due to lack of knowledge. They do not see clearly what the soldiers have been through, nor are they always capable of separating in their minds the soldiers from the actual event of war. Some believe mistakenly that the soldiers are responsible for the war or are supporters of it. This attitude was prevalent in the U.S.A. after the Vietnam War of the 1960s and early 1970s. When the soldiers returned to their homeland, they were (and still are) treated with insult and neglect. They were, quite simply, ostracized by the very people for whom they were fighting.

Soldiers are merely the pawns of the powerful. They have

little control or influence over major decisions or military strategy. They carry out orders and translate into action the theoretical desires of their superiors. For this reason, the soldiers are innocent of conceptual wrongdoing and should not be held responsible for the blunders or sins of their leaders.

Baumer knows what to expect after the war:

> . . . men will not understand us—for the generation that grew up before us, though it has passed these years with us already had a home and a calling; now it will return to its old occupations, and the war will be forgotten—and the generation that has grown up after us will be strange to us and push us aside. We will be superfluous even to ourselves . . . the years will pass by and in the end we shall fall into ruin.

But Baumer escapes this fate in death. Millions of other men, however, survived. By understanding the horrors of their experience, we can offer them love and support—necessary buffers against the nightmare of their memories. Erich Maria Remarque's novel, *All Quiet on the Western Front,* goes far in helping us accomplish this goal.

Character Sketches

Paul Baumer

Baumer is the narrator of the novel. At age 19, he enters the army, as do many of his high-school friends, after having been roused to action by an authoritarian teacher. He is a lucid man, one who is caught between the extremes of adulthood and adolescence: on the one hand, he has barely graduated from high school and has not had time to explore life, to begin planning for the future; on the other hand, he is instantly confronted with the serious demands of war, the quest for survival and the pursuit of meaning.

It is Baumer who serves as the stable figure of his troop, around whom the other characters gravitate. By this, we mean that it is Baumer's narrative that gives life to the others: we discover their stories through Baumer's eyes. And it is with Baumer that we identify the most intimately since the novel originates with him.

Baumer has had an awkward family life. Like many young boys, he has not shared a particularly warm relationship with his father, yet his mother remains an emotional inspiration to him. When Baumer goes home on leave, he has trouble identifying with his father, yet he spends many meaningful moments with his mother. He learns that she is dying of cancer, and this makes him want to spare her whatever pain he can. He knows that separating from her at the end of his leave will cause her anguish, and he attempts to shoulder responsibility for her by not becoming excessively emotional.

Baumer is something of an "Everyman," or representative of the ordinary man. His attitudes toward war, women, imprisonment, food and peace are what one might expect from a large cross-section of men his age. He yearns for peace and tries hard, in the meantime, to make life as bearable as possible. He is optimistic about life in the sense that he refuses to surrender to death. His fight for survival indicates a will to live, yet he comes to realize that the world of his superiors is not a Utopia. Rather, he sees the evils and viciousness around him and wonders what his generation will ever become.

Baumer is deeply emotional about those who have been victimized by the war. When he is forced to murder the Frenchman in order to save his own life, he spends many hours in the trench with this dying man and realizes what he has done: he has deprived another human being of living, of sharing good times with his wife and children, and so on. He regrets that the war has obliged men to carry on like predators and sees that conflict that robs people of their lives is a vile, bloody matter. Language and nationality have little to do with it: the point is, murder is murder, and Baumer despises it.

When Baumer is killed in the end, we feel a deep loss. He has struggled through months of agony and hardship. And he is within days of a free life—the armistice is about to be signed when he is shot down. Baumer, in this regard, represents everyone who is victimized by the war—victimized by the ruthless, gory mess that absurdly and painfully ends in the ruin of his country. He is kind, generous, loving and a true hero. When one reads this novel, there is little reason to think of Baumer's nationality or political stand (which rarely surfaces). He is above all a man, dedicated to peace, and caught up in someone else's battle.

Kantorek

Kantorek is the high-school teacher who persuades the young men in Baumer's class to join the army. He incites in them a fierce patriotism, which amounts to nothing short of a lie: the Germany that he portrays is one that the men discover does not exist—at least, not for them. He uses the principle of authority to gain control over them. But when they arrive in the army, they find out that life is not exciting, it is not vibrant and cheery, that there is little hope and that their futures are bleak.

Kantorek lives a dream which his generation has created in an effort to give their own lives more meaning. But when one of Baumer's class-mates rises through the ranks of the army, he finds Kantorek in one of his reserve units. This allows him the joy of punishing the teacher with treatment similar to that which the men had suffered in high school. Kantorek receives large doses of the same language that he had used on his students. Unlike Himmelstoss, Kantorek remains unredeemed by an admission of guilt or error. He is, in the minds of his former students, a condemnable, hated man.

Himmelstoss

Himmelstoss is a postman in civilian life. But in the army,

he has risen to a senior rank and is the leader of the ninth platoon in which Baumer and the men serve. His principal feature is an overbearing need to exert authority over his men, and it is this characteristic that serves as his undoing. Once they discover that his cruelty can be dealt with by passive resistance (e.g., carrying out all of his orders, but carrying them out very slowly), he sees the destructiveness of his actions. When he is reported to his superiors by the soldiers, they sympathize with the men and shock Himmelstoss into rethinking his habits.

One night, after several of the soldiers ambush Himmelstoss and give him a beating, he discovers for himself what pain the soldiers can create for people like him. Then, when he is called to action in Chapter 6, he and Baumer dive into the same dug-out, while seeking safety from the shelling. Baumer exits sometime later to resume fighting, but Himmelstoss refuses to come out. He is not the brave man he had pretended to be, and this discovery of cowardice converts him into a more honest individual. From this point on, he becomes more human with the soldiers. As a result, they accept him and treat him more kindly. Himmelstoss, then, can be seen as a man of great frustration. His life as a civilian has given him no power over himself or others, so when he achieves a powerful position in the army, he abuses this new commodity and discovers its dangers. Power becomes an obsession, a malicious toy that he manipulates recklessly and without regard for important human feelings. When his abuse backfires on him, he realizes that power is a mighty weapon and must be used with responsibility. In the end, Himmelstoss has more control by not flaunting his power than he had when he abused it.

The primary purpose of Himmelstoss in this novel is to demonstrate the volatility of power and to show that human beings respond well if they are treated well. Even in the army, where things need to be tough in order to prepare men for battle, there is always room for dignity. This, ultimately, is the lesson learned by Himmelstoss.

Stanislaus Katczinsky—'Kat'

Kat is the oldest member of Baumer's group and, as such, serves as a role model for the younger men. He is 40 years old, shrewd, experienced in life and a cunning, hard-driven man. He has an independent strain in his personality, which enables him to survive in situations where others would fall. His bold exterior, however, protects a warm sensitivity underneath, and it is this caring side of Kat that endears him to Baumer. The two become close friends in a time when emotions have little place in survival. The bodily instincts take over during battle, leaving in their wake all intellectual concerns. Certainly, there are emotional responses such as fear and panic, but these are spontaneous instincts, which occur without thought. It is during the ordeal of battle and conflict that the younger Baumer derives such stability and comfort from Kat. Kat knows how to defend himself, cook, hunt and deal with the unknown.

There is an element of paternal love in Kat's treatment of Baumer. He is perhaps the father replacement figure who derives satisfaction from knowing that he plays a major role in Baumer's army life. Fundamentally a good man, Kat is killed at the novel's end, and this leaves Baumer with one less reason to live. The survivor has died; Baumer's best friend is gone. Soon thereafter, Baumer is shot down in battle.

Style

It is never easy to discuss a novelist's style when one reads the work in translation. The words on the page are those of a translator, not of Erich Maria Remarque. Moreover, this novel is essentially a work of ideas and emotion, both of which transcend linguistics and poetics. Thought and feeling, when accurately translated into a foreign language, overcome any language barriers that may exist. They are, in fact, a universal language, which speaks directly to all people.

While it may be difficult, then, to analyze Remarque's actual style of writing, we can nonetheless make comments on his novel as a literary work. Perhaps the term "poetic realism" comes closest to articulating Remarque's manner of description. We must not assume from this term that his is a poetic work in the sense of flowers, pretty birds and softness. Rather, it is a brilliant, commanding style which appeals to every range of our emotions—and particularly to those that cause us the most pain.

Remarque writes in a realistic vein rather than in an idealistic or romantic manner. In describing a group of soldiers who, individually, form a unity, he states:

> Farther on the mist ends. Here the heads become figures; coats, trousers, and boots appear out of the mist as from a milky pool. They become a column. The column marches on, straight ahead, the figures resolve themselves into a block, individuals are no longer recognizable, the dark wedge presses onward, fantastically topped by the heads and weapons floating on the milky pool. A column—not men at all.

Here we have a poetic passage that makes full use of our imagination. We have no trouble imagining the individual men, yet we can also picture a mass of bodies marching collectively into the distance. It is realism in the style of Émile Zola—the ability to create a mob scene, while still endowing this collectivity with personality.

When Remarque describes a blast of gunfire, he says: "Balls of light rise up high above [the sky], silver and red spheres which explode and rain down in showers of red, white, and green stars.'' It is colourful and has an impact on our mind. But while this can be called poetic, it is also deeply realistic: it creates a sharp, undeniable image of chaos and havoc in the skies.

Much of this novel is ugly. It is ugly to behold yet gripping in intensity. The human predicament holds our attention as we empathize with the victims of war. But this does nothing to alter the cold, ruthless ugliness of the action. Remarque often paints in black and white. Through contrast (peace vs. war, life vs. death, etc.), he exposes the war for what it is: murder on an unforgivable scale.

The style, then, is both poetic and realistic—often colourful and almost always ugly. These are the strokes of truth that penetrate our resistance and move us right into the action. And while we may have problems in discussing Remarque's actual choice of nouns, verbs and adjectives, we can nonetheless agree on one thing: his style is honest, direct and full of meaning.

Animal Imagery

Man is an animal. But when we hear the word "animal," we think immediately of dogs, cats, horses, etc. We forget that we are intimately linked to the tree of evolution to which other animal forms also belong. We have in common with these lower forms of animals the need for food, protection against threat and so on. Survival is our means of propagating the species, so we are instinctively geared to protect ourselves in whatever ways available.

In *All Quiet on the Western Front,* there are innumerable examples of animal imagery. Remarque draws comparisons between man and other animal forms in order to bring out the most quintessential characteristics of nature. The images of animals reinforce in us such emotions as fear, pain, anxiety and our need to survive. The images also help us to see mankind in a removed, detached manner: we feel the emotions and pains of the animals, but somehow it is less appalling—though still not pleasant—to identify with such emotions in the animals.

The animal imagery brings us into contact with our own most basic, animalistic drives and urges. Below you will see a list of such images taken from the novel. When you look at them, try to identify your own reaction to the image. If you feel some emotional response, then the author has achieved his purpose:

- . . . life is simply one continual watch against the menace of death;—it has transformed us into *unthinking animals* in order to give us the weapon of instinct. . . .

- It is nothing but an awful spasm of fear, a simple *animal fear* of poking out my head and crawling on farther.

- . . . we turn into *animals* when we go up to the line, because that is the only thing which brings us through safely. . . .

- [Himmelstoss] draws up his legs, crouches back against the wall, and shows his teeth like a cur. I seize him by the arm and try to pull him up. *He barks.*

- We have become *wild beasts*. We do not fight, we defend ourselves against annihilation.

- When a shell lands in the trench we note how the hollow,

furious blast is like a blow from the paw of a raging *beast of prey*. [my italics]

The animals are sometimes compared to man, and vice versa. But their instincts are also shown to be in common with those of man. For purposes of appreciating Remarque's style, we might conclude that animal imagery is used to reinforce the essentially animalistic nature of war. It is a struggle for survival, and instinct plays a major part in avoiding death.

Selected Criticisms

The few reflections in *All Quiet* avoid taking a position on any social, religious or other issue. I only spoke about the horror, about the desperate, often raw instinct of self-preservation, about the determined force of life, that opposes death and destruction.

Erich Maria Remarque speaking to the German reporter Axel Eggebrecht ("Gespräch mit Remarque," *Die Literarische Welt.)*

Remarque's novel is a novel of pacifism, a protest against war and its devastation. It ends on a peaceful note, even a hopeful note, in spite of the epilogue of untimely death. . . . Simple pacifism, uncomplicated by considerations of economics or politics, is its central theme. War is evil; peace, by implication, is not.

Charles Olstad, *Revista de Estudios Hispánicos.*

Remarque describes the desperate heroism of soldiers who, like threatened animals, are not really fighting but are rather defending themselves against annihilation. Out of love and lust for life they kill, destroy, cause havoc among those who come running across the fields with rifles, hand grenades and flame-throwers in their hands. They become heroes not because of some nebulous ideal that a rapturous schoolmaster, in the security of a classroom, has planted in them. It is a matter of killing or being killed, or of destroying so that one may live. These are the rules of conduct for the day and the basis of heroism as Remarque sees it.

Wilhelm J. Schwarz, *War and the Mind of Germany.*

Remarque has spoken on behalf of all of us.

Ernst Toller, *Die Literarische Welt.*

To argue that Remarque is either a weak-kneed pacifist gnawing away at the nation's vitals, or a mature writer probing fearlessly at the heart of his generation's tragic fate, or again a bourgeois liberal who recognizes the disease and fails to point to a cure, is to miss the point entirely. Nor is it enough to indicate that the limitations of the work are attributable to the fact that Baumer is a relatively unsophisticated young man who would in any event be incapable of comprehending the wider historical perspective into which his individual life fits. . . .

The truth of the matter is that, in *All Quiet on the Western Front,* Remarque is proposing the view that human existence can no longer be regarded as having any ultimate meaning. Baumer and his comrades cannot make sense of the world at large for the simple reason that it is no longer possible to do so, not just for this group of ordinary soldiers, but for a substantial proportion of his entire generation. Remarque refuses to lull his reader into a false sense of security, into thinking that God is in his heaven and all is right with the world—all that is amiss is that we as individuals are too limited in vision to be able to recognize the existence of a grand design. On the contrary, he demonstrates that the holocaust of the First World War has destroyed not only any semblance of meaningfulness that the universe may seem to have possessed in the past, but that even the continuity of the individual existence has been shattered.

The largest unit of significance that remains is the individual life, sustained by the 'life force' pulsing within, which holds the individual for the brief span of his existence and then releases him into death.

Christine R. Barker and R.W. Last, Erich Maria Remarque.

Suggested Study Topics

1. What is the principal message of *All Quiet on the Western Front*?

2. When a novel achieves success all over the world, it must appeal to something deeply human in its readers. To what do you attribute the success of Remarque's novel, and how would you explain the popularity of a book that is so graphic in detail?

3. Friendship and brotherhood play an important role in this novel. Examine the relationship between Baumer and Katczinsky and explain how the two men complement one another.

4. What is the role of religion in *All Quiet on the Western Front*?

5. Explain the significance of animal imagery in this novel, with particular reference to its role in poetic realism.

6. The law of cause and effect plays a constant role in both life and this novel. To what extent does this law manifest itself in the novel?

7. In his brief introduction to the novel, Remarque states: "This book is to be neither an accusation nor a confession, and least of all an adventure. . . ." What do you suppose he meant by this?

8. What importance do you see in the character development of Himmelstoss and Kantorek? Are they similar types of people? In what ways do they differ?

9. Write a brief essay on the nature of war and show what effects war has on everyone involved.

10. Why is a novel such as *All Quiet on the Western Front* important to read? You might include in your answer some mention of the idea that war is relevant to all periods of

human civilization, that the psychological effects of conflict affect everyone (stress, tension, chaos, threat to survival, shock to international commerce, etc.). Do you see the novel as a warning against similar wars, as a method of prevention?

Appendix

World War I: Chronology of Important Events

1914

June 24	Kiel Canal widening finished
June 28	Assassination of Archduke Francis Ferdinand
July 28	Austria declares war on Serbia
July 30	Russian mobilization
Aug. 1	Germany declares war on Russia
Aug. 3	Germany declares war on France
Aug. 4	Germany attacks Belgium
	Britain declares war on Germany
Aug. 5	Austria declares war on Russia
Aug. 6	Serbia declares war on Germany
Aug. 8	Portugal declares support for Britain
Aug. 10	France declares war on Austria
Aug. 12	Britain declares war on Austria
Aug. 14	Battle of the Frontiers
Aug. 23	Battle of Mons
	Japan declares war on Austria
Aug. 25	Austria declares war on Japan
Sept. 6	Battle of the Marne
Oct. 9	Fall of Antwerp
Oct. 19	First Battle of Ypres
Oct. 29	Turkey attacks Russia
Nov. 5	France and Britain declare war on Turkey
Dec. 6	Serbs push back the Austrians

1915

Jan. 19	First Zeppelin raid on Britain
Feb. 18	First U-boat campaign
Feb. 19	Naval bombardment of Dardanelles
Apr. 22	Second Battle of Ypres: gas used
May 7	Lusitania sunk
May 23	Italy declares war on Austria
Aug. 5	Germans take Warsaw
Aug. 20	Italy declares war on Turkey
Aug. 25	Fall of Brest-Litovsk
Sept. 25	Battle of Loos
Oct. 11	Bulgaria attacks Serbia

Oct. 15	Britain declares war on Bulgaria
Oct. 16	France declares war on Bulgaria
Oct. 19	Russia and Italy declare war on Bulgaria

1916

Feb. 18	Surrender of German Cameroons
Feb. 21	Battle of Verdun
Mar. 9	Germany declares war on Portugal
Mar. 16	Austria declares war on Portugal
July 1	Battle of the Somme
Aug. 27	Rumania declares war on Austria
Aug. 28	Germany declares war on Rumania
	Italy declares war on Germany
Aug. 30	Turkey declares war on Rumania
Sept. 1	Bulgaria declares war on Rumania
Sept. 15	Tanks first used
Dec. 6	Fall of Bucharest
Dec. 7	David Lloyd George becomes Prime Minister of England

1917

Feb. 1	Second U-boat campaign
Feb. 3	U.S.A. breaks relations with Germany
Mar. 12	Russian Revolution
Mar. 14	Hindenburg Line withdrawal
Mar. 15	Czar abdicates in Russia
Apr. 6	U.S.A. declares war on Germany
Apr. 9	Battle of Arras
Apr. 16	Nivelle's offensive
June 7	Capture of Messines Ridge
June 29	Greece declares war on Germany, Turkey and Bulgaria
July 31	Third Battle of Ypres
Nov. 6	Passchendaele
Nov. 7	Vladimir Lenin seizes power in Russia
Nov. 16	Georges Clemenceau re-elected Prime Minister of France
Dec. 5	German-Russian armistice
Dec. 7	U.S.A. declares war on Austria
Dec. 9	Rumanian armistice
Dec. 15	General Russian armistice

1918

Mar. 3	Treaty of Brest-Litovsk
Mar. 21	German offensive on Somme
Mar. 29	Ferdinand Foch becomes Allied Commander-in-Chief
Apr. 9	German offensive in Flanders
May 1	First U.S.A. units in action
May 7	Treaty of Bucharest
May 27	German offensive at Soissons
July 15	Last German offensive on Marne Murder of Czar and family
July 18	Allied counter-attacks begin
Aug. 2	French retake Soissons Allied intervention in Russia
Aug. 8	Battle of Amiens: "black day of German army"
Sept. 22	Collapse of Turks in Palestine
Sept. 29	Bulgarian armistice
Oct. 30	Turkish armistice Rout of Austrians in Italy
Nov. 3	Austrian armistice
Nov. 9	Abdication of Kaiser
Nov. 11	German armistice
Nov. 21	Surrender of German fleet

1919

June 28	Treaty of Versailles (Germany)
Sept. 10	Treaty of St. Germain (Austria)
Nov. 27	Treaty of Neuilly (Bulgaria)

1920

June 4	Treaty of Trianon (Hungary)
Aug. 10	Treaty of Sèvres (Turkey)

Selected Bibliography

Army Times, Eds. *The Yanks Are Coming*. New York: Putnam, 1960.

Barker, Christine R. and R.W. Last. *Erich Maria Remarque*. New York: Barnes & Noble, 1979.

Barnett, Correlli. *The Great War*. London: Octopus Books PLC, 1979.

Blunden, Edmund. *Undertones of War*. Oxford University Press, 1956.

Cameron, James. *1914*. New York: Holt, Rinehart and Winston, 1959.

Cruttwell, C.R.M.F. *A History of the Great War, 1914-1918*. Oxford University Press, 1936.

Everett, Susanne. *World War I. An Illustrated History*. New York: Rand McNally, 1980.

Falls, Cyril. *The Great War*. New York: Putnam, 1959.

Fredericks, Pierre G. *The Great Adventure*. New York: Dutton, 1960.

Lawrence, T.E. *Seven Pillars of Wisdom*. New York: Doubleday, 1947.

Moorehead, Alan. *Gallipoli*. New York: Harper, 1956.

Oughton, Frederick. *The Aces*. New York: Putnam, 1960.

Remak, Joachim. *Saravejo*. Criterion, 1959.

Schwartz, Wilhelm J. *War and the mind of Germany*. Bern: Herbert Lang, 1975.

Wolff, Leon. *In Flanders Fields*. New York: Viking, 1958.

NOTES

NOTES

NOTES

NOTES

NOTES

NOTES

NOTES

NOTES

NOTES